Sachiyo Ishii

Sachiyo Ishii was born and raised in Japan. She was a money broker on Wall Street and in London before discovering the joy of handicraft after her second son was born. She learned dressmaking and Waldorf doll making and has been designing and creating dolls and toys ever since. She teaches knitting, doll making, wet and dry felting, sewing, crochet and spinning, among other crafts. She has authored a number of titles for Search Press and her work regularly appears in knitting magazines. Sachiyo lives in Sussex with her husband and two sons. Visit her website at www.knitsbysachi.com

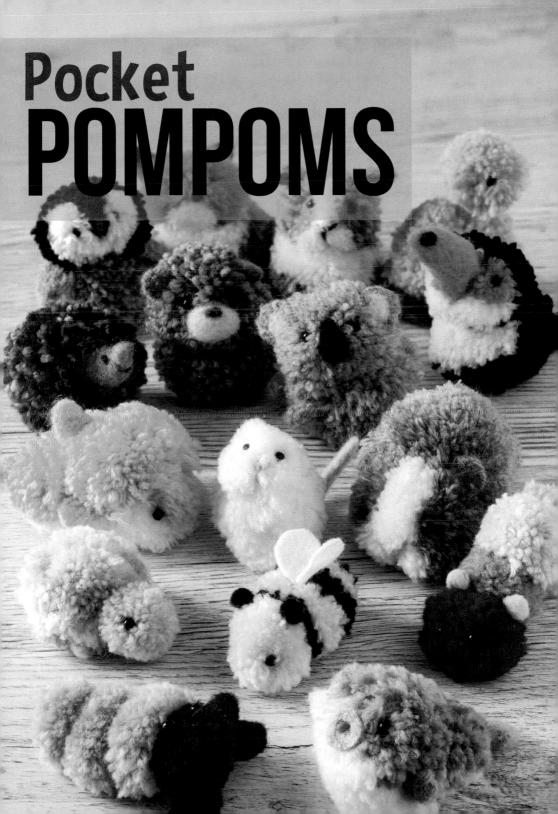

Pocket
POMPOMS

First published in 2019

Search Press Limited
Wellwood, North Farm Road
Tunbridge Wells
Kent TN2 3DR

Photographs by Stacy Grant: pages 1, 2 (except tl+bl), 3, 4
(except Toucan), 5, 6, 7, 8, 9, 11, 12, 22(m), 27, 31(b), 32,
33, 34(t), 35, 38(t+bl), 39, 40(t), 41, 42(t), 44 (except tr),
45, 46, 47, 48(t), 49, 50, 51, 52(t), 53, 54, 55, 56(t), 57, 58,
59, 60(t), 61, 62(t), 63, 64, 65, 66, 67, 68(t), 69, 70, 71, 72,
73, 74(t), 75, 76(b), 77, 78(t), 79, 80(t), 81, 82(t), 83, 84,
85(except tr), 86(t), 87, 88(br+bl), 89, 90, 91, 92(t), 93,
94, 95(t), 96, 97, 98(t), 99, 100(t), 101, 103, 104, 105, 106,
107, 108, 109(b), 111, 112.
All other photographs by Paul Bricknell at
Search Press Studios

Text copyright © Sachiyo Ishii 2019

Design copyright © Search Press Ltd. 2019

ISBN: 978-1-78221-723-7

The Publishers and author can accept no responsibility for
any consequences arising from the information, advice or
instructions given in this publication.

Readers are permitted to reproduce any of the items/patterns
in this book for their personal use, or for the purposes
of selling for charity, free of charge and without the prior
permission of the Publishers. Any use of the items/patterns
for commercial purposes is not permitted without the prior
permission of the Publishers.

Suppliers

For details of suppliers, please visit the Search Press website:
www.searchpress.com

All the step-by-step photographs in this book
feature the author, Sachiyo Ishii. No models
have been used.

You are invited to visit Sachiyo's website at:
www.knitsbysachi.com

Dedication
I would like to dedicate this book to my mum.

Acknowledgements
I would like to thank everyone on the
Search Press team, especially Katie French and
May Corfield, for helping me to create such
a wonderful book. I would also like to thank
the designers, Juan Hayward and Emma Sutcliffe,
for the beautiful layout, and the photographers,
Stacy Grant and Paul Bricknell. Thanks also go to
Clover mfg for supplying the tools.

Pocket
POMPOMS

35 LITTLE WOOLLY CREATURES TO MAKE

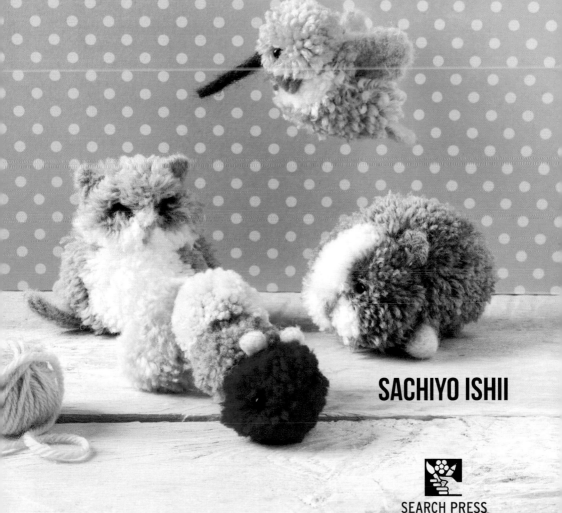

SACHIYO ISHII

SEARCH PRESS

Contents

Brown Bear, page 48

Cat, page 50

Lovebirds, page 52

Teddy Bear, page 54

Hedgehog, page 56

Koala Bear, page 58

Seal Pup, page 60

Pufferfish, page 62

Hamster, page 65

Spider, page 68

Robin, page 70

Sheep, page 72

Chicken & Chick,
page 74

Bumblebee, page 76

Ladybird, page 78

Caterpillar, page 80

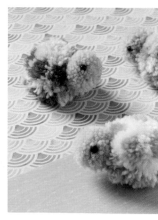

Turtle, page 82

Snail, page 86

Squirrel, page 89

Penguin, page 92

Toucan, page 95

Dolphin, page 98

Pig, page 100

Duck & Duckling,
page 102

Hummingbird, page 104

Crab & Hermit Crab,
page 106

Ostrich, page 109

Index, page 112

Introduction

I have bittersweet memories of my introduction to making pompoms. I grew up near a close cousin. She was the same age as me and we played together every day. One day, she got a set of pompom makers. They were flat ring-shaped ones and came in two sizes. I loved pompoms but had no idea how they were made. Apparently, with these small tools, you could make cute pompoms in no time. It seemed too good to be true and sounded like magic to me.

My mum was a keen knitter and had some oddments of yarn but thought pompoms were a waste of time. The yarn was expensive and she did not dare to cut it to make children's toys. My cousin was given some wool by her mum and she was allowed to make pompoms. I was so envious! I just wanted to have one for myself to hang on my school bag. Pompom animals did not exist then.

After some persuading, my cousin gave in and let me have a go, but for some reason, the yarn ended up all tangled. I had no idea how it happened but the entire ball of yarn was tangled up and my cousin was so upset that she didn't speak to me for three days.

That was my first encounter with pompom making. After that, I made pompoms by winding the yarn around my fingers or a fork, but I never thought of buying a pompom maker. It may be because it was too painful to be reminded of that incident with my cousin.

In 2017 I was commissioned to design some pompom animals for a craft magazine and was given a set of pompom makers. I could have a go, I thought. I felt a bit of pang when I cut into the thick volume of wound yarn. But once I started felting details onto it and giving it life and character, I began to really enjoy doing it. It's great fun to create things with pompoms! It has provided another dimension to my toy making. There is so much you can do with fluffy balls of yarn.

Making pompoms is an easy craft that anyone can enjoy. You can use budget yarn or any oddments in your yarn stash. If you are apprehensive about needle felting, you can always cut some ready-made felt and glue it on to make the features. One of my favourite pompoms was a school mascot that I got in America when I was an exchange student. It was fuzzy with felt feet and googly eyes stuck onto it.

Pompoms are magical. They are cute as they are, but they can also be transformed into amazing creatures that will make everyone smile.

Happy pompom making!

Tools & Materials

Materials

YARN

You can use any yarn to make pompoms. If you knit or crochet, you may already have oddments of yarn left over from previous projects and these pompoms are the perfect thing to help use up your yarn stash. I like using 4-ply (fingering) yarn, especially for smaller projects, since it gives a finer finish. If you are working with more than two colours to create a motif in a pompom, it is better to use fine yarn as well. Double knitting (DK/8-ply/light worsted) yarn gives a slightly scruffy look; however, the effect can be quite attractive for some projects, such as the Brown Bear and the Lovebirds (see below).

Pompoms can be made using synthetic or natural fibres. You may want to try some relatively cheap acrylic yarn to practise with. Cotton yarn is not suitable for making fluffy pompoms, as it may end up rather limp and looking more like a tassel. When a project requires needle felting, it is best to use yarn with a high percentage of wool. Wool felts better than other fibres, looks nice and feels great to touch.

As far as yardage goes, it is not a big consideration. However, as guidance, the yardage for the 4-ply (fingering) yarn used here is 50g per 247yd/225m; for DK (8-ply/light worsted) yarn it is 50g per 179yd/165m.

FELTING FLEECE

Also known as felting wool or wool roving, this is used to create some of the animals' features by needle felting them. Wool roving comes in different coarsenesses but for felting, Corriedale and merino are the most popular and are widely available online and from craft shops. Corriedale is a little coarser than merino and, if you are a first-timer, it may be a good choice. Wool roving can be also used to make pompoms. Experiment with it and enjoy the different effects you can achieve.

BEADS

These are used for some of the animals' eyes. You can use beads with threading holes or amigurumi safety eye beads. If the safety eye is shaped like a pin and comes with a washer, ignore the washer and glue the eyes into the pompom. I have used 2–6mm (¹⁄₁₆–¼in) beads in this book.

Safety note: if you are making a pocket pet for a small child, do not use beads, which could present a choking hazard. Instead, embroider the eyes on with yarn, or needle felt them using some felting fleece.

SEWING THREAD

Regular sewing thread is absolutely fine and this is used for attaching the eye beads.

FABRIC GLUE

I have used this to stick on small features, such as felt ears and noses.

RIBBON

This is used for the Teddy Bear project (see page 54). Feel free to use any oddments of ribbon.

READY-MADE FELT

I have used felt squares, which are widely available from craft shops. You will need only a very small amount. It does not have to be pure wool. Choose felt which is not densely woven.

READY-MADE CRAFT POMPOMS

These tiny pompoms, less than 1cm (½in) in diameter, are available from craft stores.

LIGHTWEIGHT GARDEN WIRE

This is available from garden centres or craft stores. It is used for making the Spider's legs (see page 68).

PLIERS

These are useful for cutting the garden wire.

FLORIST TAPE

This is available from garden centres or craft stores. It is used for wrapping around the wire used to make the Spider's legs.

Tools

POMPOM MAKERS

These come in many different sizes ranging from 20mm (¾in) to 115mm (4½in) in diameter. I have used 20mm (¾in), 25mm (1in), 35mm (1⅜in) and 45mm (1¾in) pompom makers. There are various types of pompom makers on the market, but I used the semicircular type with arms that pull out and away from the middle. They were easy to use, sturdy and durable.

FELTING NEEDLES

Single felting needle

Felting needles have small barbs on the end that, when stabbed through the wool fleece or yarn, catch on the scales of the fibre and push them together. The more you stab, the more the fibres mat together, slowly turning the wool into solid felt. The ends are very sharp, so take care and keep your eye on the needle at all times.

Felting needles come in different gauges. The gauge number refers to the diameter of the needle. The higher the number, the finer the needle, so a 40 gauge needle is finer than a 36 gauge. The most popular sizes are the 36, 38 and 40 triangular or star felting needles. The triangular needles have barbs on three sides, while the star needles have barbs on four sides. I like to use a fine needle, as it does not leave holes after punching with it. For the projects in this book, I have used 40 gauge triangular needle.

Multi-needle hand tools

When you want to speed up the felting process or tackle a large project, these are very helpful. I found that using multiple needles at an early stage gives stability and makes shaping easier. I work with three (or more) needles to start and move on to a single needle for the finer details.

NEEDLE FELTING MAT

I use a brush-type mat. The bristle length provides the ideal hardness and density for punching. It does not disintegrate and extends the life of felting tools and needles. I use it with a sheet of felt fabric between the brush and the project so that the fibre does not get caught in the brush. You can also use a foam felting pad if you prefer. Make sure it is at least 3cm (1¼in) deep and you should always place it on a firm surface while working and never directly on your lap. Keep lifting up your piece from time to time so that your work doesn't bond to the foam.

You do not need to felt the fibre solid while you are working on the mat. Stab just until the fibre takes shape and work some more after you attach the piece to the pompom.

SEWING NEEDLES

These are used for attaching eye beads and other accessories such as ribbon.

SCISSORS

These are essential for trimming the pompoms and cutting thread. Invest in some good-quality, sharp scissors. If the blades are blunt, the finish will not be neat. Small patchwork scissors are handy and perfect for the job.

CHENILLE NEEDLE

This type of needle has a large eye and a sharp point and is perfect for sewing the pompoms together. Projects that require two or more pompoms are connected with the same yarn used to make the pompoms

How to use the templates

For ready-made felt fabric, simply cut out your shape using the templates as you would for a sewing project.

For needle felting, however, the templates are there as an approximate guide to the size and shape. You don't need to cut anything out. Take a small amount of fleece wool for the item you are making and form it into a ball. Start needle felting it into shape and check it against the template periodically to make sure it matches. It doesn't need to match the template exactly.

Techniques

How to make pompoms

Making pompoms is fun and very easy with a pompom maker. I have used the semicircular type for this book and the instructions are written based on them. However, you can use the type you prefer. Bear in mind that, if you use a different type, you may have to improvise slightly when working with several different colours of yarn.

SEMICIRCULAR POMPOM MAKER

This kind of pompom maker is fairly sturdy and consists of two pairs of semicircular arms that fold out of a central section.

1 Open up the pompom maker, making sure the pairs of arms are lined up with each other and begin winding the yarn round one pair of arms.

2 Wrap as much yarn as you can so that the arm is full. This will help to make a nice dense pompom. Cut the yarn and tuck the end into the wound yarn – you can do this with a crochet hook if you have one.

3 Fold the first arm back to the centre.

4 Repeat step 2 for the other arm, then cut the yarn and fold it back to the centre.

5 Using a small pair of sharp scissors, cut along each half of the maker in the gap between the arm pairs. Be sure to hold the arms down so the pompom maker doesn't open up while you are cutting.

6 Check carefully that you have cut all the yarn strands.

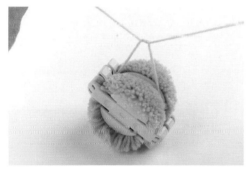

7 Take a length of yarn and wrap it around the centre of the pompom maker. Tie it securely and make a double knot. Make sure you leave long yarn ends so you can use these to attach the pompom to another one.

8 Finally, open the arms and pull the two halves apart to release the pompom. Trim off any extra long bits of yarn to shape it for a perfectly round pompom, or leave it until you attach another pompom for whatever project you are making

The finished pompom.

RING-TYPE POMPOM MAKER

This type of pompom maker is lightweight and inexpensive. It allows you to wind more yarn on than the semicircular type, but be careful not to lose or break the latches.

1 Open the rings and place them together.

2 Wind yarn around one side of the pompom maker back and forth so that it is even. Wrap it thickly to make it dense.

3 Repeat step 2 for the other side of the pompom maker.

4 Close the two halves together and push the latches down to connect the ring completely and stop it from coming apart.

5 Using a small pair of sharp scissors, cut along each half of the maker in the gap between the rings. Be careful the latch does not open while you are cutting the yarn.

6 Check carefully that you have cut all the yarn strands.

7 Take a length of yarn and wrap it around the centre of the pompom maker. Tie it securely and make a double knot. Make sure you leave long yarn ends so you can use these to attach the pompom to another one.

8 Open the latches to release the rings.

9 Remove the pompom from the maker. Trim off any extra long bits of yarn to shape it for a perfectly round pompom, or leave it until you attach another pompom for for whatever project you are making.

The finished pompom.

TRADITIONAL CARDBOARD RING METHOD

Using cardboard rings is probably the most traditional way of making pompoms and great for keeping children entertained. If you choose to use this method, please note that half of one cardboard ring corresponds to one arm of a pompom maker. Refer to the colour diagrams as well as the instructions when you make each project.

1 Cut out two identical cardboard discs for the size of pompom that you need. You can use a circular template (such as a small saucer) that is the correct size, or compasses. Cut out a smaller circle in the middle that measures half the diameter of the outer circle to make two rings. Then cut a slit in both rings.

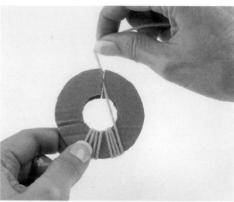

2 Hold the two cardboard rings together and wind the yarn around them.

3 To make a dense pompom, cover the cardboard evenly with plenty of yarn. Don't worry if you can't wind right up to the edge of the slit – it's more important that the yarn stays on the ring.

4 Using a small pair of sharp scissors, cut between the two cardboard rings.

5 Hold the cardboard firmly as you are cutting round the centre of the rings, as the yarn is much more likely to come loose with this type of pompom maker.

6 Take a length of yarn and push it between the two cardboard rings.

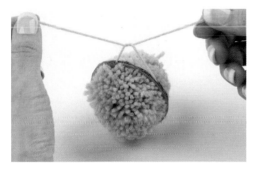

7 Tie it securely and make a double knot. Make sure you leave long yarn ends so you can use these to attach the pompom to another one.

8 Twist the cardboard in opposite directions and tear it to release the pompom. Trim off any extra long bits of yarn to shape it for a perfectly round pompom, or leave it until you attach another pompom for whatever project you are making.

The finished pompom.

DENSITY AND SIZE

For the projects in this book, it is best to make dense pompoms unless otherwise instructed. Wind as much yarn round the arms as the pompom maker allows, and be careful that the arms stay closed until you have finished tying and knotting the centre securely.

When you are working with a pompom maker that is 45mm (1¾in) or larger, wind the yarn until the arch is filled and the bottom of arm is almost level. That should provide enough density. However, if you are working with smaller pompom makers, you would want to wrap more. Try to keep yarn in place without letting it slip over the edges.

The finished size of your pompom can be controlled not only by the size of the pompom maker, but also by the volume of yarn you wind round the maker. Wrap slightly less if you want to make a smaller pompom.

For most projects I haven't indicated how many wraps you should make when winding the yarn, since you may be using yarn with a different yardage from mine. When the project specifies how many times you wrap the yarn, it relates to the weight of yarn listed in the project's materials box.

HOW TO WORK WITH SEVERAL COLOURS

There are two ways to colour pattern your pompoms: the layering method and the colour block method.

The layering method

1 Wind two layers of white yarn evenly around the first arm of the pompom maker all the way across.

2 Repeat with the blue yarn.

3 Now wind two layers of red yarn over the blue. You will find that the arm is now full. Repeat this sequence for the second arm.

4 When you cut the yarn, the white layers meet in the centre, the red layers meet on the 'outside' and the blue layers are thinner and don't meet each other.

5 Tie and knot some yarn round the centre to secure the pompom, open the arms of the pompom maker ...

6 ... and release the pompom.

The finished pompom shows two wide segments of white and red yarn and four thinner segments of blue yarn.

The colour block method

1 For this method, wrap the top third of the first arm in blue yarn, the middle third in red and the bottom in white yarn.

2 Repeat this sequence for the second arm and close both arms.

3 Cut round the centre of the pompom, tie and knot it and release it from the pompom maker.

The finished pompom shows equal segments of colour. It is a little trickier to wind the yarn using this method, as you need to prevent one yarn colour from slipping into the next. It is also possible that your pompom will be slightly smaller than it would if using the layering method.

If you wind some parts of the arm in a different colour, the colour appears in two parts symmetrically because the wrap will be separated and divided from the centre. When you make a project such as the Panda (see page 40), you need to wrap black yarn on one arm of the pompom maker only; otherwise, you end up having a second set of eyes on the back of the Panda's head!

UNDERSTANDING THE POMPOM MAKER DIAGRAMS

As I explained on page 14, I used the semicircular type of pompom maker to make all of my animals. As such, I have based all the pompom colour diagrams in the projects on that type of pompom maker. It may, therefore, be useful to explain in detail how the colour daigrams should be interpreted, depending on which type of pompom maker you are using.

If we look at the Dog project on pages 28–31, this project uses two colours and gives instructions for how to wind the yarn onto the arms of the pompom maker.

First, wind a layer of white yarn onto the first arm. Then wind the top third with three more layers of white yarn. Then cover the whole arm with brown yarn until it is full.

For the second arm, wind it with brown yarn until it is full.

Pompom maker diagrams

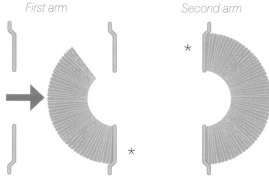

First arm

Second arm

When the instructions refer to the 'hinge end' of the pompom maker, it refers to the parts of the diagram above marked ★.

This pompom arm represents the first arm in the diagrams.

This pompom arm represents the second arm in the diagrams.

If you are using the semicircular type of pompom maker as I did for this book, the hinge is on the bottom of the first arm and the top side of the second arm, since the arms open outwards on both sides (see opposite).

However, if you are using the ring-type pompom maker, the hinge corresponds to the bottom of both the first and second arm; if you are using cardboard rings, the hinge area corresponds to the point opposite the slot (see below).

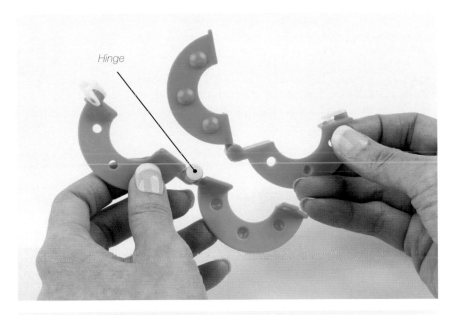

Hinge

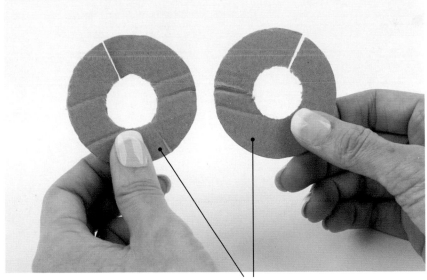

Hinge area corresponds to the point opposite the slot

How to make the animals

This is a step-by-step guide to making the pompom animals. It covers such things as joining the pompoms together, needle felting and attaching features such as the muzzle and ears, attaching the eye beads and also embroidering on the features. Many of these techniques can used for all the pompom creatures in the book.

MAKING THE MONKEY

Materials

To make one adult:

10g (⅓oz) 4-ply (fingering) yarn in soft brown
Two 4mm (⅛in) black beads
Beige cotton thread
Small amount of beige felting fleece
Small amount of 2-ply (lace weight) brown yarn

To make one baby:

Small amount of 4-ply (fingering) yarn in soft brown
Two 2mm (¹⁄₁₆in) black beads
Beige cotton thread
Small amount of beige felting fleece
Small amount of 2-ply (lace weight) yarn in brown

Tools

25mm (1in), 35mm (1⅜in) and 45mm (1¾in) pompom makers
Patchwork scissors
Single needle felting tool
Needle felting mat
Sewing needle

Size

Adult Monkey: 6cm (2¼in); Baby Monkey: 4cm (1½in)

Templates

Adult Monkey: Ear and Muzzle

Baby Monkey: Ear and Muzzle

Leave loose fibres where dotted lines are shown.

1 For the Adult Monkey, make one head pompom using the 35mm (1⅜in) pompom maker, and one body pompom using the 45mm (1¾in) maker, both using soft brown yarn. Leave long tail ends when you tie the pompoms round the centre.

2 Connect the two pompoms with one of the tail ends of yarn, pulling it tightly to connect them securely.

3 Once connected, the head will sit seamlessly on top of the body. There will inevitably be a few stray lengths of yarn.

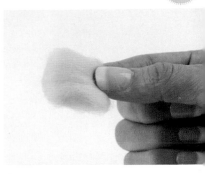

4 Trim any longer pieces of yarn to tidy up the pompoms. It helps to roll them in your hands a few times as you are trimming, to settle the yarn.

5 The result will be a nice, neat elongated ball shape. It doesn't need to be overly neat.

6 To make the muzzle, take a small amount of beige felting fleece and roll it into 2 x 3cm (¾ x 1¼in) loose flat shape.

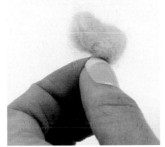

7 Place it on a felting mat and stab the fleece with a felting needle. Check it against the template to get the shape and size approximately the same and lift the fleece time to time so that it doesn't stick to the mat.

8 The fleece will knit together and become a solid shape, but don't needle felt it too much – leave some loose fibres around the edges. The base of the muzzle should be wider than the top.

9 Now attach the muzzle to the front of the face by felting the loose fibres into the pompom.

10 To make the ears, take a small amount of felting fleece and roll it into a 1cm (⅜in) width. Work as for the face, felting it into shape and using the template periodically to check the size and shape.

11 Leave some loose fibres trailing from the inner edge. Repeat for the other ear.

12 Attach both ears to the side of the head by needle felting the loose fibres into the pompom.

13 Position the ears as evenly as you can.

14 To make the eyes, thread a needle with some black cotton and bring it from the back of the head through to the top of the muzzle section.

15 Thread a bead onto the needle and take it back through the head from front to back.

16 Bring the needle back to the front and thread the second bead onto the needle.

17 Take the needle through to the back of the head and fasten off securely.

18 Thread your needle with a length of 2-ply (lace weight) brown yarn to embroider the nose and mouth. Bring the needle to the front, through the muzzle and make two small, vertical straight stitches for nostrils.

19 Bring the needle back to the front, to one side and take it across to the other side to make the mouth, pushing it through to the back. Bring it back to the centre front, just above the long stitch you made for the mouth, and then push it back in just underneath the stitch to pull it down slightly into a smile. Fasten off securely.

The finished monkey.

Baby Monkey

Work as for the Adult Monkey, using a 25mm (1in) pompom maker for the head and a 35mm (1⅜in) pompom maker for the body.

MAKING THE DOG

This step-by-step guide to making the pompom Dog involves some
colour work, so this is described with the use of diagrams of the pompom
makers (see below) and how to wind the different colours onto it.

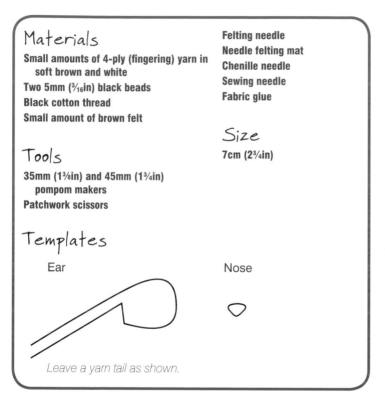

Materials

Small amounts of 4-ply (fingering) yarn in
   soft brown and white
Two 5mm (³⁄₁₆in) black beads
Black cotton thread
Small amount of brown felt

Tools

35mm (1³⁄₈in) and 45mm (1³⁄₄in)
   pompom makers
Patchwork scissors

Felting needle
Needle felting mat
Chenille needle
Sewing needle
Fabric glue

Size

7cm (2³⁄₄in)

Templates

Ear   Nose

Leave a yarn tail as shown.

Pompom maker diagrams

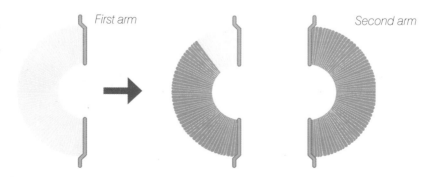

First arm   *Second arm*

1 For the head, wind the first arm with white yarn using a 35mm (1⅜in) pompom maker. Then wind the top third with three more layers of white yarn.

2 Start covering the white yarn in soft brown yarn.

3 Wind with the soft brown yarn until the arm is full. Use soft brown yarn to wrap the second arm until it is full.

4 Cut the yarn all the way round, tie it securely round the centre and make a double knot, leaving a long yarn tail.

5 Release it from the pompom maker and you will see that you have a white face at the front of the head. For the body, make a pompom in soft brown yarn with the 45mm (1¾in) pompom maker.

6 Connect the head and body pompoms using the yarn tail. Draw the yarn tight to connect two pompoms securely.

7 Trim the connected pompoms to shape so you have a nice neat head and body.

8 Gather the white yarn towards the centre of the face and needle felt it to shape the muzzle.

9 You will see that the area has become denser in appearance than it was before.

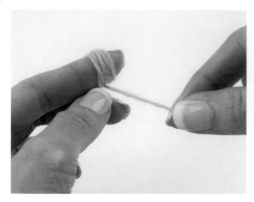

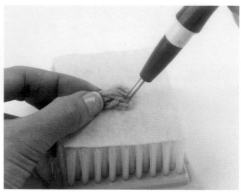

10 To make the ears, wind some soft brown yarn around your forefinger about ten times, leaving a long tail end.

11 Release it and place it onto a felting mat. Needle felt it with a multi-head tool until the yarn fibres are knitted together, comparing it to the shape of the template every so often to check the size and shape are correct.

12 You will have a nice dense triangular ear shape. Repeat steps 10 and 11 to make the second ear.

13 Thread the tail end of yarn attached to one of the ears onto a needle and attach it to the side of the head.

14 Take your needle in and out of the head pompom, going through the centre, to secure the ear and then fasten off.

15 Repeat to attach the second ear.

16 Attach the eye beads (see steps 14–17 of the Monkey on page 26). Cut out a nose from brown felt using the template and attach with fabric glue.

The finished dog.

Fox

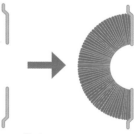

Materials

Small amounts of 4-ply (fingering) yarn in
   orange and white
Two 4mm (⅛in) black beads
Black cotton thread
Small amount of black and white felting fleece
Small piece of dark brown felt

Tools

25mm (1in), 35mm (1⅜in) and 45mm (1¾in)
   pompom makers
Patchwork scissors
Felting needle
Needle felting mat
Chenille needle
Sewing needle
Fabric glue

Size

6.5cm (2½in)

Instructions

1 For the head, make a pompom using the 35mm (1⅜in)
pompom maker. Wind the top third of the first arm in
white so that it is full. Then wind the rest in orange (see
below). Wind the second arm in orange only (see pages
20–21 for information on working with colours). Tie the
centre and finish making the pompom.

First arm   *Second arm*

2 To make body pompom, take the 45mm (1¾in)
pompom maker and wind four layers across in white yarn,
then cover this with orange yarn (see below). The arm
should be full. Wind the second arm in orange yarn only.
Tie the centre and finish making the pompom. Leave a
long yarn tail.

First arm

3 Connect the head and body pompoms using the
yarn tail. Position the white areas in the centre of both
pompoms, using the photograph for guidance. Draw the
yarn tight to connect the two pompoms securely and trim
the head and body to shape.

4 To make the ears, wind some orange yarn around your forefinger about fifteen times, release it and place it onto a felting mat. Stab it with your felting needle until the yarn is bound together and the ear matches the shape of the template.

5 Take a small amount of black fleece and felt it to the tip of the ear (see the template for guide lines). Then felt a small amount of white fleece to the inside of the ear, as shown in the photograph on page 34. Repeat steps 4 and 5 for the other ear, then attach the ears to the head using the yarn tails (see page 30 for instructions on attaching features).

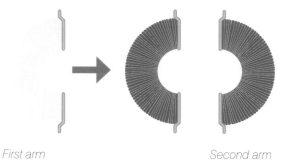

First arm *Second arm*

6 To make the tail, take the 25mm (1in) pompom maker and wind one arm in white and the other in orange. Make the pompom as usual, trim to shape and attach the tail to the body.

7 Attach the eye beads using black cotton thread (see page 26 for instructions on attaching eyes).

8 For the nose, cut a piece of dark brown felt to the shape of the template and glue it onto the muzzle.

9 Finally, needle felt around the eyes a little to flatten the yarn, which makes the eyes stand out.

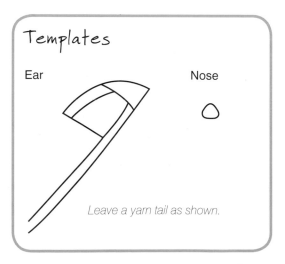

Templates

Ear   Nose

Leave a yarn tail as shown.

Bunny

Instructions

1 For the head, make a pompom using the 35mm (1⅜in) pompom maker. Wind across the first arm with two layers of white yarn, then wind just the top third of the arm with three more layers of white. Using grey yarn, wrap it over the white yarn until the arm is full. Wind the second arm in grey yarn only (see below). See pages 20–21 for instructions on working with colours. Tie the centre, and finish making the pompom.

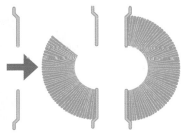

First arm   *Second arm*

2 For the body, make a pompom using the 45mm (1¾in) pompom maker. Wind the top two thirds of the first arm in white and the rest in grey. Wind the second arm in grey only. Tie the centre and finish making the pompom. Leave a long yarn tail.

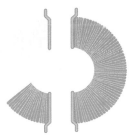

3 Connect the head and body pompoms using the yarn tail. Position the white areas in the centre of both pompoms, using the photograph for reference. Draw the yarn tight to connect the two pompoms securely. Trim the Bunny to shape.

Materials

Small amounts of 4-ply (fingering) yarn in grey, white and dark brown
Two 5mm (³⁄₁₆in) black beads
Black cotton thread

Tools

35mm (1⅜in) and 45mm (1¾in) pompom makers
Patchwork scissors
Felting needle
Needle felting mat
Chenille needle
Sewing needle

Size

7cm (2¾in)

Template

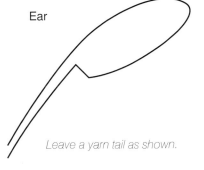

Ear

Leave a yarn tail as shown.

4 For the ears, wind some grey yarn around two fingers fifteen times, release and place it onto a felting mat. Stab with a felting needle until the yarn knits together, matching the ear to the shape of the template. Attach the ears to the head, using the yarn tails (see page 30 for instructions on making and attaching features with yarn). Use the photograph, right, for reference.

5 Attach the eye beads (see page 26 for instructions on attaching eyes).

6 Gather the white yarn towards the centre of the face and needle felt it to shape the muzzle. You don't need to felt it so that it becomes solid, just until the muzzle begins to take shape (see steps 8–9 on page 29).

7 To embroider the nose and mouth, thread a needle with some dark brown yarn, insert it through the back of the head and take it out at the front. Make a loose horizontal stitch, then bring the needle out halfway along this stitch and just above it (7a). Make a vertical stitch for the mouth, hide the yarn end inside the pompom and fasten off (7b).

The Bunny's nose is a downward-curving horizontal stitch and the mouth is simply a vertical stitch going down from the centre of the nose (see left).

Panda

Instructions

Mummy Panda

1 For the head, make a pompom using the 35mm (1⅜in) pompom maker. Wind the first arm with two layers of white yarn and then add black yarn top and bottom, as indicated in the diagram below, winding the yarn about fifteen times. Then cover the whole arm with white yarn until it is full. Wind the second arm in white yarn only. Tie the centre and finish making the pompom.

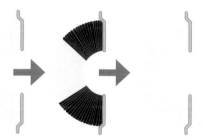

First arm

2 For the body, make a pompom using the 45mm (1¾in) pompom maker. Wind the top half of the first arm in black yarn. Wind the rest in white yarn until it is full. Wind the second arm in white yarn only. Tie the centre and finish making the pompom. Leave a long yarn tail.

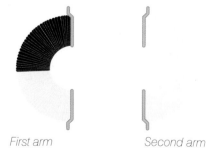

First arm   *Second arm*

3 Connect the two pompoms using the yarn tail. Draw the yarn tight to connect the pompoms securely. Trim the Panda to shape.

Materials

To make both:

Small amounts of 4-ply (fingering) yarn in white and black

Small amount of black felting fleece or small piece of black felt

Two 5mm (³⁄₁₆in) and two 4mm (⅛in) black beads

Fabric glue (optional)

Tools

25mm (1in), 35mm (1⅜in) and 45mm (1¾in) pompom makers

Patchwork scissors

Felting needle

Needle felting mat

Chenille needle

Sewing needle

Size

Mummy Panda: 6.5cm (2½in); Baby Panda: 5.5cm (2¼in)

Templates

Mummy Panda   Baby Panda

Ear   *Ear*

Leave yarn tails as shown.

Nose   *Nose*

4 Using the tip of a felting needle, tidy up the yarn around the eyes, separating the black and white yarn for a neat appearance.

5 For the ears, wind some black yarn around your forefinger ten times, release and place it onto a felting mat. Stab it with a felting needle until the yarn knits together, matching the ear to the shape of the template. Repeat for the other ear. Attach them to head, using the yarn tails (see page 30 for instructions on making and attaching features with yarn).

6 For the nose, take a small amount of black felting fleece, roll it between your fingers and place it onto a felting mat. Stab it with a felting needle until the fleece knits together, matching the nose to the shape of the template. Attach it to face, working into the loose fibre. Alternatively, cut a piece of black felt to match the template and glue it to the face.

7 Attach the eye beads (see page 26 for instructions on attaching eyes).

Baby Panda

1 For the head, make a pompom using the 25mm (1in) pompom maker. Wind the first arm with two layers of white yarn and then add black yarn top and bottom, as indicated in the diagram for the Mummy Panda, winding the yarn about seven times. Then cover the whole arm with white yarn until it is full. Wind the second arm in white yarn only. Tie the centre and finish making the pompom.

2 For the body, make a pompom using the 35mm (1⅜in) pompom maker. Wind half of the first arm in black yarn. Wind the rest in white yarn until it is full. Wind the second arm in white yarn only. Tie the centre and finish making the pompom.

3 For the rest, work as for the Mummy Panda.

Mouse

Materials

Small amounts of 4-ply (fingering) yarn in white or soft brown, and pink

Small amount of beige or brown felting fleece

Two 4mm (⅛in) black beads

Black cotton thread

Tools

25mm (1in) and 35mm (1⅜in) pompom makers

Patchwork scissors

Felting needle

Needle felting mat

Chenille needle

Sewing needle

Size

4cm (1½in)

Templates

Tail   Ear

Leave loose fibres where dotted lines are shown.

Instructions

1 For the head, make a pompom using the 25mm (¾in) pompom maker and white or soft brown yarn.

2 For the body, make a pompom using the 35mm (1⅜in) pompom maker and white or soft brown yarn, leaving a long yarn tail.

3 Connect the head and body pompoms with the yarn tail. Draw the yarn tight to connect the two pompoms securely. Trim the Mouse to shape.

4 To make the tail, place a length of beige or brown felting fleece about 1 x 6cm (½ x 2¼in) long on the mat, stabbing it with a needle as you roll it into a stick shape (see below). Lift the fleece time to time so that the piece doesn't stick to the mat. Work until it is fairly firm, matching it to the template. Leave some fibre trailing from one end.

5 Attach the tail to the body by needle felting the loose fibres into the body pompom (see right).

6 For the ears, take a small amount of white or brown fleece, roll it into a small ball of 1cm (½in) or so and stab it with a needle. Work until it is fairly firm, matching it to the template. Leave some fibre trailing from the flat edge. Attach the ears to the head by felting the loose fibres into the pompom.

7 Attach the eye beads (see page 26 for instructions on attaching eyes).

8 To embroider the nose and mouth, follow step 7 on page 38 for the Bunny.

Owl

Materials

To make both:

Small amounts of 4-ply (fingering) yarn in brown, sandy brown, white and dark brown

Two 6mm (¼in) and two 4mm (⅛in) black beads

Black cotton thread

Small piece of yellow felt

Yellow cotton thread

Tools

25mm (1in), 35mm (1⅜in) and 45mm (1¾in) pompom makers

Patchwork scissors

Felting needle

Needle felting mat

Chenille needle

Sewing needle

Size

Mummy Owl: 6.5cm (2½in); Baby Owl: 5.5cm (2¼in)

Instructions

Mummy Owl

1 To make the pompom for the head, take the 35mm (1⅜in) pompom maker and wind the top 5mm (¼in) of the first arm in brown until it is full. Then wind one layer of the sandy brown yarn next to it. Add white yarn as indicated in the diagram below, winding it about 20 times. Cover the white yarn with sandy brown yarn so that the arm is full. Wind the second arm with sandy brown yarn only and finish the pompom.

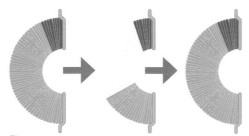

First arm

2 To make the body pompom, take the 45mm (1¾in) pompom maker and wind one layer of brown yarn. Add dark brown yarn, winding twice over the same place and then leaving a space (this will create the dark brown dots), repeating this several times across the arm. Then cover this with one layer of brown yarn. Repeat these two layers about five times, so that the arm is full.

3 Connect the head and body pompoms with a loose end of yarn from one of the pompoms. Draw the yarn tight to connect the two pompoms securely and trim the head and body to shape.

4 Cut a piece of yellow felt to the shape of the large beak template. Using a fine sewing needle and yellow cotton thread, attach the beak to the face by threading through the flat edge of the beak and sewing it into a downward curve, and fasten off securely.

5 Attach the eye beads (see page 26 for instructions on attaching eyes).

6 Trim the top of head to shape the ears. Using a felting needle, needle felt around the eyes to make them stand out.

Baby Owl

Work as for the Mummy Owl, using a 25mm (1in) pompom maker for the head and a 35mm (1⅜in) pompom maker for the body. When making the pompom for the head, wind the white yarn about ten times to make the white eye circles. Use the small beak template.

Templates

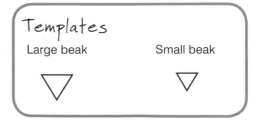

Large beak

Small beak

Brown bear

Instructions

1 Using the 35mm (1⅜in) pompom maker, make two pompoms for the head and body using brown yarn. Leave a long yarn tail on one of the pompoms.

2 Attach the two pompoms to each other using the yarn tail. Draw the yarn tight to connect the two pompoms securely. Trim the head and body to shape.

3 To make the ears, wind some brown yarn around your forefinger ten times, release and place it onto the felting mat. Stab with a felting needle until the yarn knits together and the ear matches the shape of template, leaving a long strand. Repeat for the second ear, then attach them to head, using the long strand (see page 30 for instructions on making and attaching features with yarn).

4 For the muzzle, take a small amount of cream felting fleece and roll it into 2 x 3cm (¾ x 1¼in) loose, flat ball. Stab with felting needle to shape it into the template. Lift the fleece from time to time so that the piece doesn't stick to the mat. Leave some fibres trailing from the back.

5 Attach the muzzle to the head by felting the loose fibres into the pompom.

6 Take a small amount of dark brown felting fleece and roll it between your fingers. Felt it into the muzzle to make the nose.

7 Attach the eye beads (see page 26 for instructions on attaching eyes).

Materials

Small amount of DK (8-ply/light worsted) yarn in brown
Small amounts of cream and dark brown felting fleece
Two 4mm (⅛in) black beads
Black cotton thread

Tools

35mm (1⅜in) pompom maker
Patchwork scissors
Felting needle
Needle felting mat
Chenille needle
Sewing needle

Size

5cm (2in) high

Variation

If you wish to make a fluffier looking bear, you can use fleecy yarn to make the pompoms (see below). I used brown felting fleece for the muzzle.

Templates

Ear   Muzzle

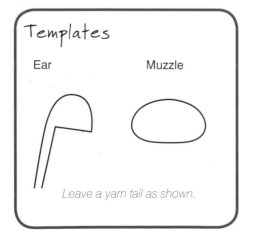

Leave a yarn tail as shown.

Cat

Instructions

1 Using the 35mm (1⅜in) pompom maker, make a pompom for the head. Wind the top third of the first arm in white until it is full. Wind the rest in grey. Wind the second arm in grey only (see pages 20–21 for instructions on working with colours). Finish making the pompom.

First arm   *Second arm*

2 Using the 45mm (1¾in) pompom maker, make the body pompom. Wind the top half of the first arm in white until it is full. Wind the rest in blue. Wind the second arm in blue only. Finish making the pompom, leaving a long yarn tail.

3 Connect the head and body pompoms with the long yarn tail. Draw the yarn tight to connect the two pompoms securely. Trim the Cat to shape.

4 To make the ears, wind some grey yarn around your forefinger ten times, release and place it onto a felting mat. Make sure you leave a long yarn tail. Stab it with a felting needle until the yarn knits together and the ear matches the shape of template. Repeat for the second ear. Attach the ears to the head, using the long tail end and a chenille needle (see page 30 for instructions on making and attaching features with yarn).

5 Using dark brown yarn, embroider the eyes with a curved backstitch. Using pink yarn, embroider a Y-shape for the nose and mouth (see step 7 for the Bunny on page 38).

6 To make the tail, wind some blue yarn around three fingers four times, release and place it onto a felting mat. Stab it with a felting needle and make it into a sausage shape, matching the size and shape to the template. Attach the tail to the body with the yarn tail and a chenille needle, as for the ears, threading it through the centre of the pompom.

Materials

Small amounts of 4-ply (fingering) yarn in blue, white, dark brown and pink

Tools

35mm (1⅜in) and and 45mm (45mm (1¾in) pompom makers
Patchwork scissors
Felting needle
Needle felting mat
Chenille needle
Sewing needle

Size

7cm (2¾in)

Templates

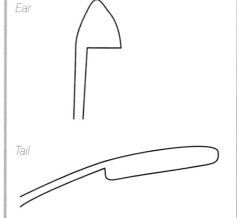

Ear

Tail

Leave yarn tails as shown.

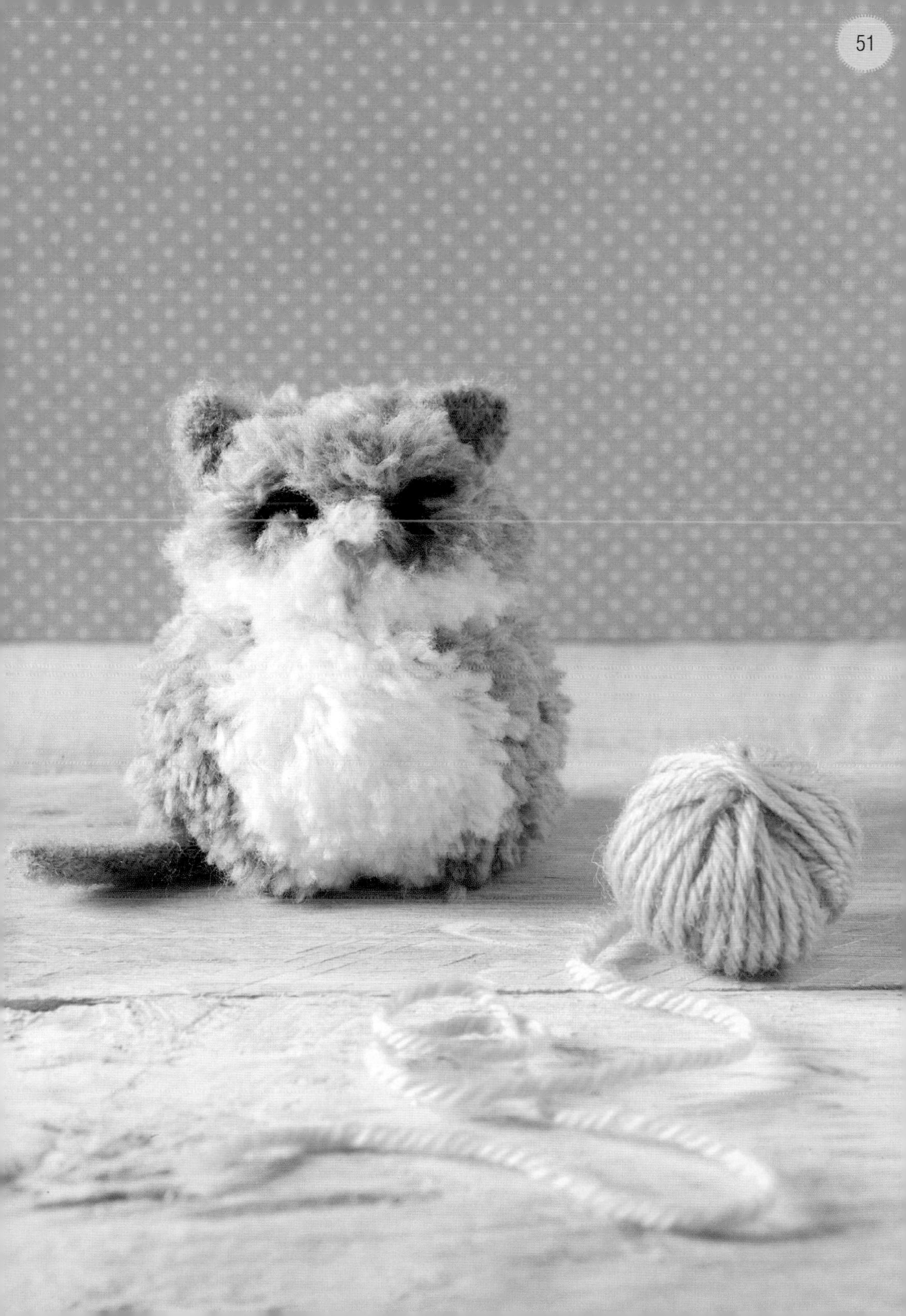

Lovebirds

Instructions

1 For the head, make a pompom using the 20mm (¾in) pompom maker in either blue or pink yarn.

2 For the body, make a pompom using the 25mm (1in) pompom maker. Wind the first arm in white and the second arm in blue or pink. Leave a long yarn tail.

3 Connect the head and body pompoms using the long yarn tail. Draw the yarn tight to connect the two pompoms securely. Trim the Lovebird to shape.

4 To make the tail, wind blue or pink yarn around your forefinger ten times, release and place it onto a felting mat. Stab it with a felting needle, matching the shape to the tail template. Use a multi-needle felting tool if you have one. Then attach the tail to the body (see page 30 for instructions on making and attaching features with yarn).

5 Attach the eye beads (see page 26 for instructions on attaching eyes).

6 For the beak, cut out a piece of yellow felt to the shape of the template. Using a sewing needle and some thread, attach the beak to the face by threading through the flat edge of the beak, sewing it into a downward curve, and fasten off securely.

Materials

To make both:

Small amounts of 4-ply (fingering) yarn in blue, pink and white

Four 4mm (⅛in) black beads

Black cotton thread

Small amount of yellow felt

Tools

20mm (¾in) and 25mm (1in) pompom makers

Patchwork scissors

Felting needle

Needle felting mat

Chenille needle

Sewing needle

Size

3.5cm (1½in)

Templates

Beak   Tail

Leave a yarn tail as shown.

Teddy Bear

Instructions

1 For the head and body, make two pompoms using brown yarn and the 35mm (1⅜in) pompom maker. Leave a long yarn tail on one of the pompoms.

2 Attach the two pompoms to each other using the yarn tail. Draw the yarn tight to connect the two pompoms securely.

3 For the legs, make two pompoms using brown yarn and the 20mm (¾in) pompom maker. Leave long yarn tails. Attach the legs to the body using the yarn tails. Draw the yarn tight to connect them securely. Trim the Teddy Bear to shape.

4 For the ears, wind some brown yarn around your forefinger ten times, release and place it onto a felting mat. Stab with a felting needle until the yarn knits together and matches the template. Attach the ears to the head, using the yarn tail (see page 30 for instructions on making and attaching features with yarn).

5 To make the arms, wind some brown yarn around your forefinger eight times, release and place it onto a felting mat. Work as for the ears, then attach the arms securely to the body.

6 For the muzzle, take a small amount of sandy brown felting fleece and roll it into 2 x 3cm (¾ x 1¼in) loose flat ball. Stab it with a felting needle until it matches the shape of the template. Lift the fleece from time to time so that the piece doesn't stick to the mat. Leave some fibres trailing from the back.

7 Attach the muzzle to the face by needle felting the loose fibres into the pompom.

8 Using dark brown yarn, embroider a nose and mouth onto the muzzle. Make a few horizontal stitches for the nose, tapering at the top to give an approximate triangular shape, and one long straight stitch from the bottom of the nose to make the mouth.

9 Attach the eye beads (see page 26 for instructions on attaching eyes).

10 Make a bow with the ribbon and sew it to the front of the bear using the cotton thread.

Materials

Small amounts of 4-ply (fingering) yarn in brown and dark brown
Small amount of sandy brown felting fleece
Two 4mm (⅛in) black beads
Black cotton thread
20cm (8in) length of 5mm (¼in) wide red ribbon
Red cotton thread

Tools

20mm (¾in) and 35mm (1⅜in) pompom makers
Patchwork scissors
Felting needle
Needle felting mat
Chenille needle
Sewing needle

Size

7cm (2¾in)

Templates

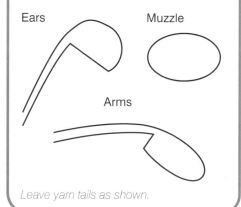

Ears

Muzzle

Arms

Leave yarn tails as shown.

Hedgehog

Instructions

Note: you can make the hedgehog in three different sizes.

1 To make the body, make a pompom using the 25mm (1in), 35mm (1⅜in) or 45mm (1¾in) pompom maker, depending on which size of hedgehog you are making. Wind dark brown yarn onto the first arm, adding small amounts of soft brown yarn here and there at random. Make sure the first arm is full, then repeat for the second arm. Finish making the pompom.

2 To make the snout, take a small amount of felting fleece and roll it into 2cm, 3cm or 4cm (¾in/1¼in/1½in) ball. Stab with a felting needle, shaping it to the template. Lift the fleece from time to time so that the piece doesn't stick to the mat. Allow more fleece towards the body end to make it into a cone shape. Leave some fibres trailing from the wider end.

3 Attach the snout to the body by felting the loose fibres into the pompom.

4 Using some dark brown yarn 4-ply (fingering) yarn, embroider the eyes with French knots and make the mouth with a backstitch.

Materials

To make a set of three:

12g (½oz) DK (8-ply/light worsted) yarn in dark brown and a small amount in brown

Small amount of 4-ply (fingering) yarn in dark brown

Small amount of sandy brown fleece

Fabric glue

Tools

25mm (1in), 35mm (1⅜in) and 45mm (1¾in) pompom makers

Patchwork scissors

Felting needle

Needle felting mat

Chenille needle

Sewing needle

Size

Small: 4.5cm (1¾in); Medium: 5.5cm (2¼in); Large: 6.5cm (2½in)

Templates

Snout

Large

Medium

Small

Leave loose fibres where dotted lines are shown.

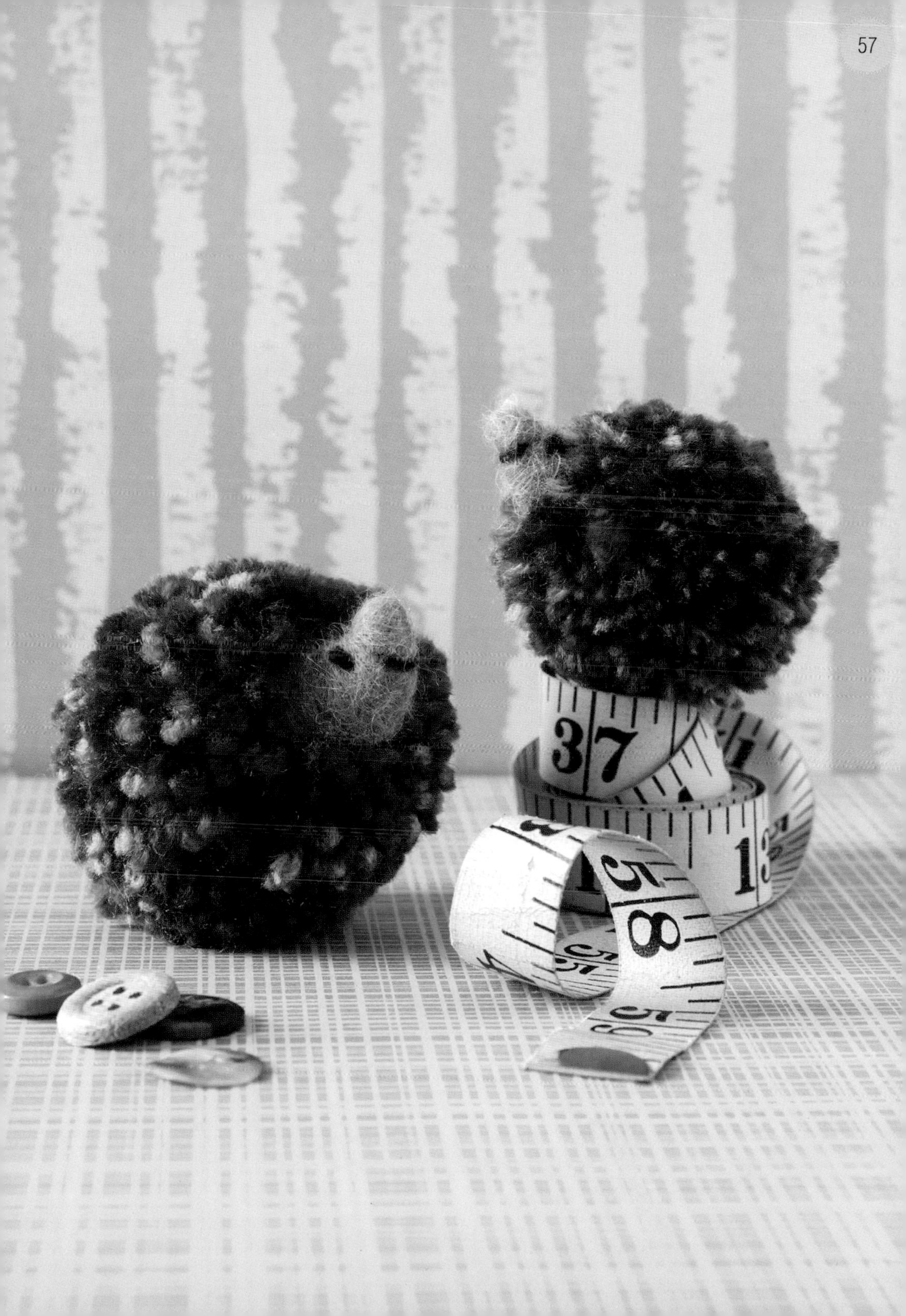
37

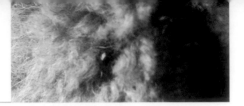

Koala Bear

Instructions

1 For the head, make a pompom using the 35mm (1⅜in) pompom maker and grey yarn.

2 For the body, make a pompom using the 45mm (1¾in) pompom maker and grey yarn. Leave a long yarn tail.

3 Connect the head and body pompoms using the yarn tail. Draw the yarn tight to connect the pompoms securely. Trim the head and body to shape.

4 To make the ears, wind some grey yarn around your forefinger ten times, release and place it onto a felting mat. Stab with a felting needle until the yarn knits together, matching it to the shape of the template. Take a small amount of white fleece and needle felt it to the centre of the ear. Attach the ears to the head, using the yarn tail (see page 30 for instructions on making and attaching features with yarn).

5 Attach the eye beads (see page 26 for instructions on attaching eyes).

6 For the nose, take a small amount of dark brown felting fleece and roll it into a 2 x 3cm (¾ x 1¼in) loose, flat ball. Stab it with a felting needle. Lift the fleece from time to time so that the piece doesn't stick to the mat. Allow more fleece at the bottom edge to make it into a cone shape. Work until it is fairly firm. Leave some loose fibres trailing from the back of the piece (see steps 8–9 on page 25). Attach the nose to the face, working the loose fibres into the pompom.

7 For the arms, wrap some grey yarn around two fingers eight times, release and place it onto a felting mat. Stab it with a needle, felting it into a sausage shape. Repeat for the second arm. Attach the arms to the body using the yarn tails.

Materials

Small amounts of 4-ply (fingering) yarn in grey and white

Small amounts of white and dark brown felting fleece

Two 5mm (³⁄₁₆in) black beads

Black cotton thread

Tools

35mm (1⅜in) and 45mm (1¾in) pompom makers

Patchwork scissors

Felting needle

Needle felting mat

Chenille needle

Sewing needle

Fabric glue

Size

6cm (2¼in)

Templates

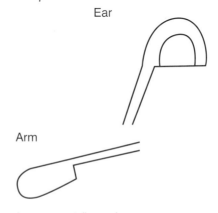

Ear

Arm

Leave yarn tails as shown.

Seal Pup

Instructions

1 For the head, make a dense pompom using the 35mm (1⅜in) pompom maker and white yarn.

2 For the body, make a dense pompom using the 45mm (1¾in) pompom maker and white yarn. Leave a long yarn tail.

3 Connect the two pompoms using the yarn tail. Draw the yarn tight to connect the two pompoms securely. Trim the Seal Pup to shape.

4 For the muzzle, take a small amount of white felting fleece and roll it into 2 x 3cm (¾ x 1¼in) loose ball. Stab with a felting needle, matching it to the shape of the template. Lift the fleece from time to time so that the piece doesn't stick to the mat. Leave some fibres trailing from the back.

5 Attach the muzzle to the face, working the loose fibres into the pompom.

6 Attach the eye beads (see page 26 for instructions on attaching eyes).

7 For the flippers, wind some white yarn around two fingers fifteen times, release and place it onto a felting mat. Stab with a felting needle until the yarn knits together and the flipper matches the shape of template. Repeat for the other flipper, then attach them to body using the yarn tail (see page 30 for instructions on making and attaching features with yarn).

8 For the hind flippers, repeat step 7 and make two flippers. Attach them by felting the two together at the tip. Attach them to the tail end, using the long yarn tail.

9 Using dark brown yarn, embroider the nose and mouth with backstitches. Draw some dots on the muzzle with a black felt-tip pen.

Materials

Small amount of 4-ply (fingering) yarn in white and dark brown
Small amount of white felting fleece
Two 4mm (⅛in) black beads
Black cotton thread

Tools

35mm (1⅜in) and 45mm (1¾in) pompom makers
Patchwork scissors
Felting needle
Needle felting mat
Chenille needle
Sewing needle
Black felt-tip marker pen

Size

6cm (2¼in)

Templates

Front flippers

Muzzle

Back flippers

Leave yarn tails as shown.

Pufferfish

Instructions

Large Pufferfish

1 For the head and body, make a pompom using the 45mm (1¾in) pompom maker. Wind the first arm in grey across one layer. Then continue winding in grey, adding blue here and there at random. Wind until the arm is half full. Cover with white yarn until the arm is full. Wind the second arm, using white yarn only. Finish making the pompom, leaving a long yarn tail.

First arm   *Second arm*

2 For the tail end, make a pompom using the 25mm (1in) pompom maker. Work as for the head and body pompom.

3 Connect the head and body with the tail end pompom using the yarn tail. Draw the yarn tight to connect the two pompoms securely. Trim the Pufferfish to shape.

4 For the side fins, wind some grey yarn around your forefinger ten times, release and place it onto a felting mat. Stab it with a felting needle until the yarn knits together, matching the fin to the shape of the template. Repeat for the other fin. Attach them to the body, using the yarn tails (see page 30 for instructions on making and attaching features with yarn).

5 For the tail fin, wind some grey yarn around your forefinger twelve times and work as for step 4.

6 Attach the eye beads (see page 26 for instructions on attaching eyes).

7 For the mouth, cut out some green felt to the shape of the template and glue it to the face.

Materials

To make both:

Small amounts of 4-ply (fingering) yarn in white, grey and blue

Two 5mm (³⁄₁₆in) and two 4mm (⅛in) black beads

Black cotton thread

3 x 3cm (1¼ x 1¼in) green felt

Fabric glue

Tools

20mm (¾in), 25mm (1in), 35mm (1³⁄₈in) and 45mm (1¾in) pompom makers

Patchwork scissors

Felting needle

Needle felting mat

Chenille needle

Sewing needle

Size

7cm (2¾in)

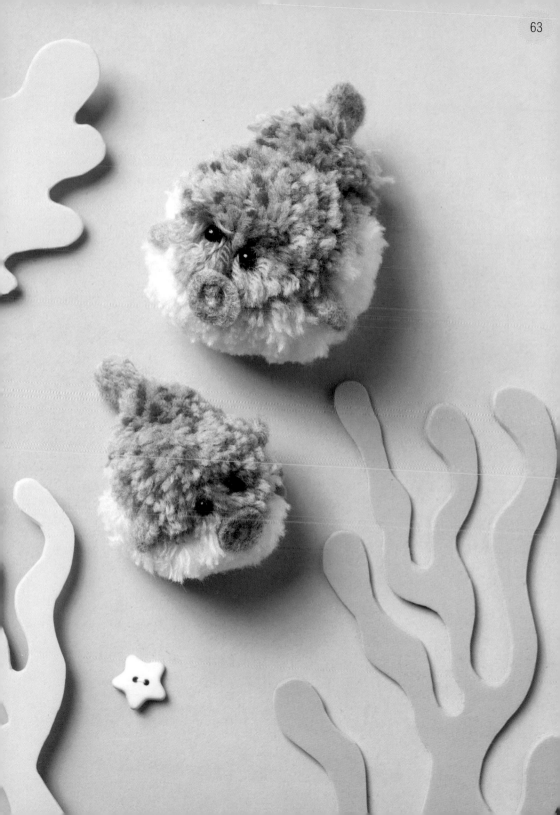

Small Pufferfish

Work as for the Large Pufferfish, using the 35mm
(1⅜in) pompom maker for the head and body
pompom and the 20mm (¾in) pompom maker for
the tail end pompom.

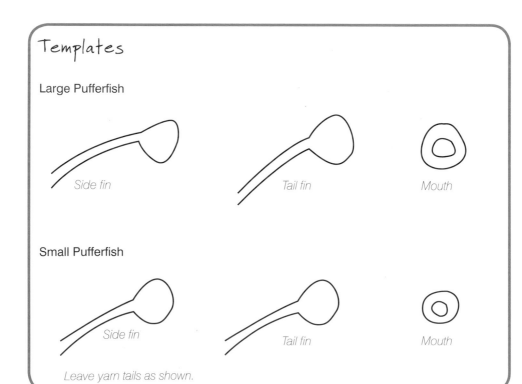

Templates

Large Pufferfish

Side fin

Tail fin

Mouth

Small Pufferfish

Side fin

Tail fin

Mouth

Leave yarn tails as shown.

Hamster

Instructions

1 For the head, make a pompom using the 35mm (1⅜in) pompom maker. Wind the first arm with two layers of white yarn and carry on winding the top third with three more layers. Cover the white yarn with brown yarn and wind until the arm is full. Wind the top third (the hinge end) of the second arm in white yarn and the rest in brown yarn (see diagrams below). See pages 20–21 for information on working with colours. Finish making the pompom.

2 For the body, make a pompom using the 45mm (1¾in) pompom maker. Wind both arms in brown yarn. Finish the pompom, leaving a long yarn tail.

3 Attach the head and body pompoms to each other using the yarn tail. Draw the yarn tight to connect the two pompoms securely. Trim the head and body to shape.

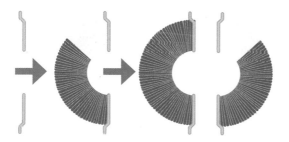

First arm

Second arm

Materials

Small amounts of 4-ply (fingering) yarn in brown, white and pink
Small amount of beige felting fleece
Two 5mm (³⁄₁₆in) black beads
Black cotton thread

Tools

35mm (1⅜in) and 45mm (1¾in) pompom makers
Patchwork scissors
Felting needle
Needle felting mat
Chenille needle
Sewing needle

Size

7cm (2¾in)

4 For the ears, wind some brown yarn around your forefinger ten times, release and place it onto a felting mat. Stab it with a felting needle until the yarn knits together, matching it to the shape of the template. Attach the ears to the head, using the yarn tail (see photograph right, and page 30 for instructions on making and attaching features with yarn).

5 Attach the eye beads (see page 26 for instructions on attaching eyes).

6 For the legs, take a small amount of beige felting fleece and felt it into tiny sausage shape. Leave loose fibres trailing from one end. Repeat, making three more legs. Attach the legs to the body, working the loose fibres into the pompom with a felting needle.

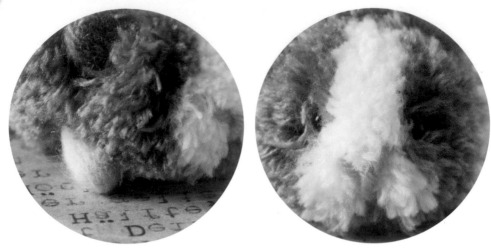

7 Embroider the nose and mouth using pink yarn (see step 7 for the Bunny on page 38). Simply make a loose horizontal stitch, then bring the needle out halfway along this stitch and just above it. Make a vertical stitch for the mouth, pulling the yarn down into a Y-shape. Hide the yarn end inside the pompom and fasten off.

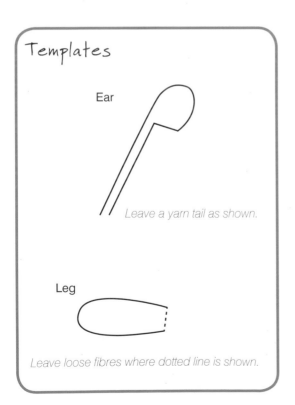

Templates

Ear

Leave a yarn tail as shown.

Leg

Leave loose fibres where dotted line is shown.

Spider

Instructions

1 For the body, make a pompom using the 25mm (1in) pompom maker. Wrap the first arm with a layer of black yarn, then wind it with white yarn, as indicated in the diagram below, about eight times. Wind the second arm with black yarn only. Tie the centre and finish making the pompom. Trim the spider to shape.

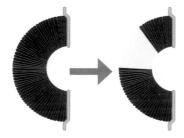

First arm

2 Attach the eye beads in the centre of the white circles (see page 26 for instructions on attaching eyes).

3 Cut four lengths of lightweight wire to about 7cm (2¾in) and pass them through the centre of the body so there is an even length of wire on each side. Bend the legs so that they curve, using the photograph below for guidance.

4 Finally, wrap the florist wire carefully with florist tape.

Materials

To make one:

Small amounts of 4-ply (fingering) yarn in black and white

Two 4mm (⅛in) black beads

Black cotton thread

20cm (8in) of lightweight wire

Black florist tape

Tools

25mm (1in) pompom maker

Patchwork scissors

Felting needle

Chenille needle

Sewing needle

Pliers

Paper scissors (to cut florist tape)

Size

3.5cm (1½in)

Robin

Instructions

Mummy Robin

1 For the body, make a pompom using the 35mm (1⅜in) pompom maker. Wind the first arm in orange-red yarn until it is almost full, then wrap the last layer using brown yarn. Wrap the second arm using brown yarn only. Finish making the pompom.

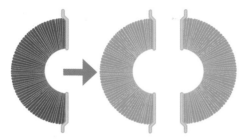

First arm   *Second arm*

2 For the wings, wind some brown yarn around your forefinger ten times, release and place it onto a felting mat. Stab it with a felting needle until the yarn knits together, matching the wing to the shape of the template. Repeat for the other wing. Attach them to the body, using the yarn tails (see page 30 for instructions on making and attaching features with yarn).

3 For the tail, work in the same way as for the wings, winding the yarn around your forefinger fifteen times.

4 Attach the eye beads (see page 26 for instructions on attaching eyes).

5 For the beak, cut some dark brown felt to the shape of the template. Using a fine sewing needle and black cotton thread, attach the beak to the face by threading through the flat edge of the beak and sewing it into a downward curve, and fasten off securely.

Baby Robin

Work as for the Mummy Robin, using the 25mm (1in) pompom maker. For the wings, wind some brown yarn around your forefinger five times, and for the tail, eight times.

Materials

To make both:

Small amounts of 4-ply (fingering) yarn in brown and orange red
Two 4mm (⅛in) and two 2mm (¹⁄₁₆in) black beads
Black cotton thread
Small amount of dark brown felt

Tools

25mm (1in) and 35mm (1⅜in) pompom makers
Patchwork scissors
Felting needle
Needle felting mat
Chenille needle
Sewing needle

Size

Mummy Robin: 3.5cm (1½in); Baby Robin: 2.5cm (1in)

Templates

Mummy Robin

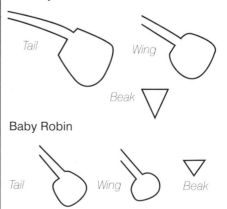

Tail   *Wing*

Beak

Baby Robin

Tail   *Wing*   *Beak*

Leave yarn tails as shown.

Sheep

Instructions

1 For the head, make a pompom using the 35mm (1⅜in) pompom maker and fleecy white yarn. Tie the centre of the pompom using DK (8-ply/light worsted) white yarn, leaving a long yarn tail.

2 For the body, make two pompoms using the 45mm (1¾in) pompom maker and fleecy white yarn. Tie the centre of the pompom using DK (8-ply/light worsted) white yarn again. Attach the two pompoms to each other using the yarn tail. Draw the yarn tight to connect the two pompoms securely.

3 Attach the head pompom to the front of the body, using the yarn tail on the head pompom. To position it, use the photograph as guidance. Draw the yarn tight to connect the two pompoms securely. Trim the Sheep to shape.

4 For the face, take a small amount of white felting fleece and roll it into a 3 x 3cm (1¼ x 1¼in) ball. Stab it with a felting needle. Allow more fibre towards one end, making it into a cone shape. Lift the fleece from time to time so that the piece doesn't stick to the mat. Leave some loose fibres trailing from the wider end.

5 For the ears, roll up a small amount of white felting fleece. Stab it with a felting needle, matching it to the size of the template. Leave some loose fibres trailing from the flat edge. Attach the face and ears to the head, working the loose fibres into the pompom.

6 For the legs, take a small amount of beige felting fleece and felt it into a small sausage shape, matching it to the template. Leave some loose fibres trailing from the flat edge. Repeat for the other three legs. Attach the legs to the body, working the loose fibres into the pompom.

7 Attach the eye beads (see page 26 for instructions on attaching eyes).

8 Embroider the nose and mouth using dark brown yarn (see step 7 on page 38 for the Bunny). Simply make a loose horizontal stitch, then bring the needle out halfway along this stitch and just above it. Make a vertical stitch for the mouth, pulling the yarn down into a Y-shape (see photograph below). Hide the yarn end inside the pompom and fasten off.

Materials

13g (½oz) of fleecy DK (8-ply/light worsted) yarn in white (25g per 85m yarn used for the sample)

Small amount of DK (8-ply/light worsted) yarn in white to tie pompom centre

Small amount of 4-ply (fingering) yarn in dark brown

Small amount of white and beige felting fleece

Two 4mm (⅛in) black beads

Black cotton thread

Tools

35mm (1⅜in) and 45mm (1¾in) pompom makers

Patchwork scissors

Felting needle

Needle felting mat

Chenille needle

Sewing needle

Size

7cm (2¾in)

Templates

Face

Ear

Leg

Leave loose fibres where dotted lines are shown.

Chicken & Chick

Instructions

Chicken

1 For the body, make a pompom using the 45mm (1¾in) pompom maker and white yarn. Tie the centre and finish making the pompom. Trim the Chicken to shape.

2 For the beak, take a small amount of orange felting fleece and roll it into 2 x 2cm (¾ x ¾in) loose flat ball. Stab it with a felting needle, matching it to the shape of the template. Lift the fleece from time to time so that the piece doesn't stick to the mat. Leave some fibres trailing from the flat edge. Attach the beak by felting the loose fibres into the pompom.

3 For the wattle, take a small amount of red felting fleece and roll it into a cone shape. Felt it to half the shape of the template. Make another piece and felt them together at the pointed ends, leaving some fibre trailing from the tip. Attach the wattle by working the loose fibres into the pompom.

4 For the crest, work as for the wattle to make three individual parts and felt them together at the pointed ends. Leave some fibres trailing from the tip. Attach it to body by felting the loose fibres into the pompom.

5 Attach the eye beads (see page 26 for instructions on attaching eyes).

Chick

1 For the body, make a pompom using the 25mm (1in) pompom maker and soft yellow yarn. Tie the centre and finish making the pompom. Trim the Chick to shape.

2 For the beak, work as for the Chicken. Attach the beak to the body by felting the loose fibres into the pompom.

3 Attach the eye beads in the same way as for the Chicken.

Materials

Small amount of DK (8-ply/light worsted) yarn in white and soft yellow
Small amount of orange and red felting fleece
Two 5mm (³⁄₁₆in) and two 4mm (⅛in) black beads
Black cotton thread

Tools

25mm (1in) and 45mm (1¾in) pompom makers
Patchwork scissors
Felting needle
Needle felting mat
Chenille needle
Sewing needle

Size

Chicken: 5cm (2in); Chick: 3cm (1¾in)

Templates

Beak

Wattle

Crest

Leave loose fibres where dotted lines are shown.

Bumblebee

Instructions

1 For the head, make a dense pompom using the 20mm (¾in) pompom maker and yellow yarn. Leave a long yarn tail.

2 For the body, make two pompoms in exactly the same way using the 25mm (1in) pompom maker. Wind the top and bottom third of each arm in black, and the middle in yellow (see below). Tie the centre and finish the pompom. Leave a long yarn tail.

First arm　　　*Second arm*

3 Connect the three pompoms with the yarn tails, using the photograph for guidance on the colours. Draw the yarn tight to connect the pompoms securely. Trim the Bumblebee to shape.

4 Attach the eye beads (see page 26 for instructions on attaching eyes).

5 Using a felting needle, tidy up the yarn and separate the colours from each other for neat a appearance.

6 For the wings, cut some white felt to the shape of the template. Using white cotton thread, attach them to the back of the body by sewing down the centre line and threading through the middle of the pompom.

7 Glue the ready-made black pompoms to the top of the head on either side (see photograph right).

Materials

Small amounts of 4-ply (fingering) yarn in yellow and black
Two 4mm (⅛in) black beads
Black cotton thread
Two 6mm (¼in) ready-made black craft pompoms
3 x 4cm (1¼ x 1½in) white felt fabric
White cotton thread
Fabric glue

Tools

20mm (¾in) and 25mm (1in) pompom makers
Patchwork scissors
Felting needle
Needle felting mat
Chenille needle
Sewing needle

Size

4.5cm (1¾in)

Template

Wings

Ladybird

Instructions

1 For the head, make a pompom using the 20mm (¾in) pompom maker and black yarn.

2 For the body, make a pompom using the 25mm (1in) pompom maker. For the first arm, wind one layer of black yarn and then cover this with one layer of red yarn, making about 30 wraps. To add dots, wrap some black yarn several times on the same spot. Repeat twice more, making sure the black yarn is evenly spaced (see below). Cover with red yarn until the arm is full.

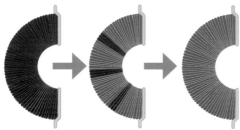

First arm

Materials

Small amounts of 4-ply (fingering) yarn in red and black

Tools

20mm (¾in) and 25mm (1in) pompom makers
Patchwork scissors
Felting needle
Needle felting mat
Chenille needle

Size

4cm (1½in)

3 For the second arm, wind one layer of black yarn and then cover this with red yarn until the arm is full. Tie the centre using black yarn, and finish the pompom. Leave a long yarn tail.

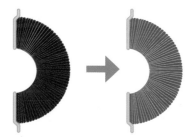

Second arm

4 Attach the two pompoms to each other using the yarn tail. Draw the yarn tight to connect them securely. Trim the ladybird to shape.

5 Using a felting needle, tidy up the yarn and separate the colours from each other to make the dots stand out neatly.

Caterpillar

Instructions

1 For the head and body, make five pompoms, one in each colour, using the 25mm (1in) pompom maker. Leave long yarn tails.

2 Connect the five pompoms to one another using the yarn tails. Draw the yarn tight to connect them securely and give the body a curve. Trim the Caterpillar to shape.

3 Attach the eye beads (see page 26 for instructions on attaching eyes).

4 Glue the ready-made craft pompoms to the head.

Materials

Small amounts of 4-ply (fingering) yarn in red, and four shades of green
Two 4mm (⅛in) black beads
Black cotton thread
Small yellow ready-made craft pompoms
Fabric glue

Tools

25mm (1in) pompom maker
Patchwork scissors
Felting needle
Needle felting mat
Chenille needle
Sewing needle

Size

8cm (3¼in)

Turtle

Materials

Small amounts of 4-ply (fingering) yarn in
sandy-brown, pale yellow and green/green
and blue/green and purple (depending on
which turtle you are making)
Two 4mm (⅛in) black beads
Cotton thread

Tools

20mm (¾in) and 35mm (1⅜in)
pompom makers
Patchwork scissors

Felting needle
Needle felting mat
Chenille needle
Sewing needle

Size

4cm (1½in)

Template

Leg

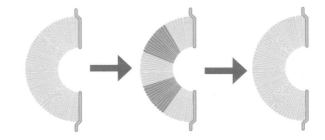

Leave a yarn tail as shown.

Instructions

Note: you can make the turtle in
different colour combinations; this is
for the pale yellow and green turtle.

1 For the head, make a pompom
using the 20mm (¾in) pompom
maker and sandy-brown yarn.

2 For the body, make a pompom
using the 35mm (1⅜in) pompom
maker. Wind a layer of pale yellow
across the first arm. To add the spots
for the shell, wind some green yarn
in one area about 25 times, leaving
gaps in between. Repeat for a second
area of green. Fill the gaps with pale
yellow yarn. Then cover the whole
arm in pale yellow until it is full.

First arm

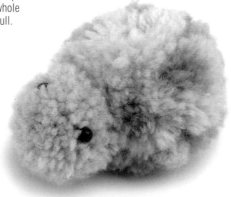

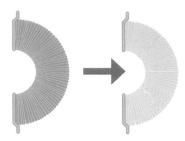

Second arm

3 Wind the second arm with green yarn. Use yellow yarn for the last layer. Tie the centre and finish the pompom. Leave a long yarn tail.

4 Connect the two pompoms using the yarn tail. Draw the yarn tight to connect them securely. Trim the Turtle to shape.

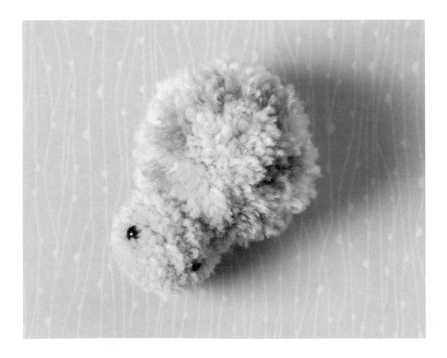

5 Using a felting needle, tidy up the yarn and separate the colours from each other to make the spots stand out neatly (see right).

6 For the legs, wind some sandy-brown yarn around your forefinger eight times, release and place it onto the felting mat. Stab it with a felting needle until the yarn knits together and the leg matches the shape of the template. Leave a long yarn tail. Repeat for the other three legs. Attach them to the body, using the yarn tails (see page 30 for instructions on making and attaching features with yarn).

7 Attach the eye beads (see page 26 for instructions on attaching eyes).

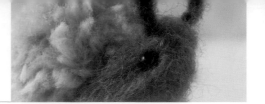

Snail

Materials

To make one:

Small amount of 4-ply (fingering) yarn in soft yellow, yellow-green, pink or blue and brown
Two 2mm (¹⁄₁₆in) black beads
Black cotton thread
Small amount of brown felting fleece

Tools

25mm (1in) pompom maker
Patchwork scissors
Felting needle(s)
Needle felting mat
Sewing needle

Size

6cm (2¼in)

Instructions

1 For the shell, make a pompom using the 25mm (1in) pompom maker and the yarn colour of your choice. Tie the centre and finish the pompom. Leave a long yarn tail.

2 For the body, place some brown felting fleece about 6cm (2¼in) long on the felting mat. Stab it with a felting needle (see above). Use a multi-needle tool, if you have one, to make it quicker.

3 Roll it into a curved cone shape, allowing more fleece at one end. Lift the fleece from time to time so that the piece doesn't stick to the mat.

4 Work until it is fairly firm and matches the template.

Template

Body

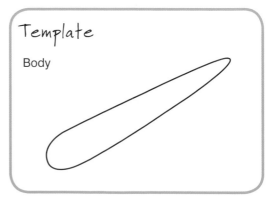

5 To make the snail's eye stalks, thread a needle with some dark brown yarn and take it through from the bottom of the body to the top of the head, just to one side.

6 Make two small loops with the yarn on either side of the head.

7 Felt the loops into sticks on the felting mat.

8 Attach the eye beads (see page 26 for instructions on attaching eyes) and then thread the yarn end from the shell pompom through the snail's body a few times to attach the shell to the body.

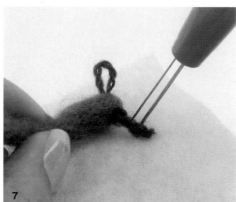

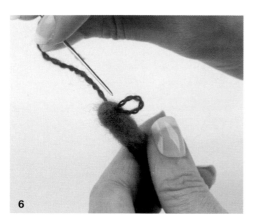

Squirrel

Instructions

1 For the head, make a pompom using the 35mm (1⅜in) pompom maker. Wind the top half of the first arm in white yarn and the bottom half in orange yarn until it is full. Wind the second arm in orange only. Tie the centre and finish the pompom. Leave a long yarn tail. See pages 20–21 for instructions on working with colours.

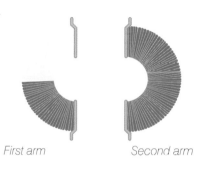

First arm   *Second arm*

2 For the body, make a pompom using the 45mm (1¾in) pompom maker. Wind the top two-thirds of the first arm in white yarn and the rest in orange. Wind the second arm in orange yarn only. Wind until the arms are full. Tie the centre and finish the pompom. Leave a long yarn tail.

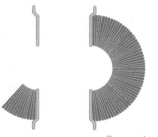

First arm   *Second arm*

3 Attach the head and body pompoms to each other using the yarn tail and referring to the photographs for guidance on colour positioning. Draw the yarn tight to connect the two pompoms securely. Trim the Squirrel to shape.

Materials

Small amounts of 4-ply (fingering) yarn in orange, white and dark brown
Two 5mm (³∕₁₆in) black beads
Black cotton thread

Tools

35mm (1⅜in) and 45mm (1¾in) pompom makers
Patchwork scissors
Felting needle
Needle felting mat
Chenille needle
Sewing needle

Size

6cm (2¼in)

Template

Ear

Leave a yarn tail as shown.

4 For the ears, wind some orange yarn around your forefinger ten times, release and place it onto a felting mat. Stab it with a needle until the yarn knits together and the ear matches the shape of template. Repeat for the other ear. Attach them to the head using the yarn tails (see photograph, right, and page 30 for instructions on making and attaching features with yarn).

5 Attach the eye beads (see page 26 for instructions on attaching eyes). Embroider the mouth and nose using dark brown yarn, with a curved horizontal stitch for the nose and a vertical stitch for the mouth.

6 For the tail, make two pompoms using the 25mm (1in) pompom maker and orange yarn. Leave long yarn tails. Attach the two pompoms to each other securely using one of the yarn tails. Use the other yarn tail to attach the tail to the body pompom (see below).

Penguin

Materials

Small amounts of 4-ply (fingering) yarn in black and white

Small amount of DK (8-ply/light worsted) yarn in grey

Two 4mm (⅛in) black beads

Black cotton thread

Small amount of black felt

Tools

35mm (1⅜in) and 45mm (1¾in) pompom makers

Patchwork scissors

Felting needle

Needle felting mat

Chenille needle

Sewing needle

Size

7cm (2¾in)

Instructions

1 For the head, make a pompom using the 35mm (1⅜in) pompom maker. Wind the top half of the first arm in black yarn across three layers. Wind three layers of white yarn over the bottom half of the arm. Leaving the top 5–8mm (¼in) free, wind four layers of white yarn over the rest. Finally, wind two layers of black yarn over the whole of the top half, including the top 5–8mm (¼in). Wind the second arm in black yarn only. Tie the centre and finish making the pompom.

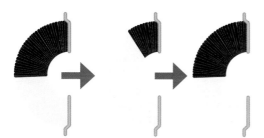

First arm

2 For the body, make a pompom using the 45mm (1¾in) pompom maker and grey yarn. Tie the centre and finish making the pompom. Leave a long yarn tail.

3 Attach the two pompoms to each other using the yarn tail. Draw the yarn tight to connect the two pompoms securely. Trim the Penguin to shape.

4 Using a felting needle, tidy up the yarn and separate the colours from each other for a neat appearance.

5 For the wings, wind some grey yarn around two fingers ten times, release and place it onto a felting mat. Stab it with a felting needle until the yarn knits together, matching it to the shape of the template. Repeat for the other wing. Attach the wings to the body, using the yarn tail (see page 30 for instructions on making and attaching features with yarn).

6 For the beak, cut a piece of black felt to the shape of the template. Using a fine sewing needle and some black cotton thread, attach the beak to the face by threading through the flat edge of the beak, sewing it into a downward curve, and fasten off securely.

7 Attach the eye beads (see page 26 for instructions on attaching eyes).

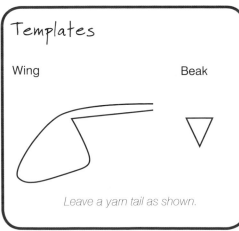

Templates

Wing   Beak

Leave a yarn tail as shown.

Toucan

Instructions

1 For the head, make a pompom using the 35mm (1⅜in) pompom maker. For the first arm, wind the top third in black, the middle third in orange and the bottom third in white. Wind each colour until the arm is full. Tie the centre and finish the pompom.

First arm   *Second arm*

2 For the body, make a pompom using the 45mm (1¾in) pompom maker. For the first arm, wind the top half in white yarn and the bottom half in black yarn until the arm is full. Wind the second arm in black yarn only, until it is full. Tie the centre and finish the pompom. Leave a long yarn tail.

First arm   *Second arm*

3 Attach the head and body pompoms to each other using the yarn tail. Refer to the photograph for guidance on colour positioning. Draw the yarn tight to connect the two pompoms securely. Trim the Toucan to shape.

Materials

Small amounts of 4-ply (fingering) yarn in black, orange and white
Small amounts of orange and black felting fleece
Two 4mm (⅛in) black beads
Black cotton thread

Tools

35mm (1⅜in) and 45mm (1¾in) pompom makers
Patchwork scissors
Felting needle
Needle felting mat
Chenille needle
Sewing needle

Size

12cm (4¾in) from beak to tail

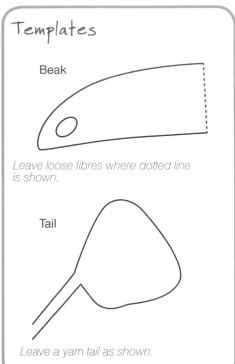

Templates

Beak

Leave loose fibres where dotted line is shown.

Tail

Leave a yarn tail as shown.

4 For the beak, place a length of orange fleece about 6cm (2¼in) long on the felting mat, roll it from one edge and stab it with a needle. Allow more fleece at the base of the beak, working it into a curved cone shape. Lift the fleece from time to time so that the piece doesn't stick to the mat. Work until it is fairly firm and matches the shape of the template. Leave some fibres trailing from the straight edge. Add a small amount of black felting fleece to the tip of the beak and felt it firmly (see above). Repeat on the other side.

5 Attach the beak to the face, felting the loose fibres at the base into the pompom head.

6 Attach the eye beads (see page 26 for instructions on attaching eyes).

7 For the tail, wind some black yarn around two fingers fifteen times, release and place it onto a mat. Stab it with a needle until the yarn knits together and the tail matches the shape of the template. Attach it to the body using the yarn tail (see photograph right, and page 30 for instructions on making and attaching features with yarn).

Dolphin

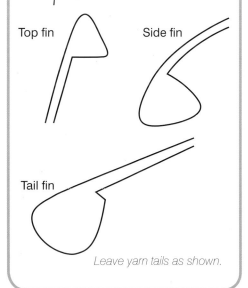

Instructions

Dolphin

1 For the body, make a pompom using the 45mm (1¾in) pompom maker. Wind the top 1cm (½in) of the first arm in white yarn and the rest in sky-blue yarn until the arm is full. Wind the bottom 1cm (½in) (hinge end) of the second arm in white yarn and the rest in sky-blue yarn until the arm is full. The colour proportions are done in the same way as for the Squirrel's head on page 89. Tie the centre and finish the pompom. Leave a long yarn tail.

2 For the tail, make a pompom using the 35mm (1⅜in) pompom maker. Work as for the body pompom. Tie the centre and finish the pompom.

3 Attach the body and tail pompoms to each other using the yarn tail. Draw the yarn tight to connect the two pompoms securely. Trim the Dolphin to shape.

4 For the top and side fins, wind some sky-blue yarn around your forefinger ten times, release and place it onto a felting mat. Stab it with a felting needle until the yarn knits together and the fin matches the shape of the template. Make one top fin and two side fins. Attach the fins to the body, using a yarn tail and a chenille needle (see page 30 for instructions on making and attaching features with yarn).

5 For the tail fin, wind some sky-blue yarn around two fingers fifteen times and work as for step 4. Repeat to make a second fin. Attach them to each other by felting them together at the base. Then attach them to the tail, using the yarn tails.

6 Attach the eye beads (see page 26 for instructions on attaching eyes).

Materials

Small amounts of 4-ply (fingering) yarn in sky blue and white
Two 5mm (³⁄₁₆in) black beads
Black cotton thread

Tools

35mm (1⅜in) and 45mm (1¾in) pompom makers
Patchwork scissors
Felting needle
Needle felting mat
Chenille needle
Sewing needle

Size

9cm (3½in)

Templates

Top fin

Side fin

Tail fin

Leave yarn tails as shown.

Pig

Instructions

1 For the head, make a pompom using the 35mm (1⅜in) pompom maker and pale pink yarn. Tie the centre and finish the pompom.

2 For the body, make a pompom using the 45mm (1¾in) pompom maker and pale pink yarn. Tie the centre and finish the pompom. Leave a long yarn tail.

3 Attach the two pompoms to each other using the yarn tail. Draw the yarn tight to connect the two pompoms securely. Trim the Pig to shape.

4 For the ears, take a small amount of beige felting fleece and roll it into 2 x 2cm (¾ x ¾in) flat, loose ball. Stab it with a felting needle, matching the shape to the template. Lift the fleece from time to time so that the piece doesn't stick to the mat. Leave some fibres trailing from the straight edge. Repeat for the second ear.

5 Attach the ears to the head, working the loose fibres into the pompom.

6 For the arms, take a small amount of beige felting fleece and roll it into 1 x 2cm (½ x ¾in) fairly tight ball. Stab it with a felting needle and make it into a sausage shape. Leave some loose fibres at the shoulder edge. Repeat for the second arm.

7 Attach the arms to the body, working the loose fibres into the pompom.

8 For the snout, work as for the ears using beige felting fleece and make a flat oval shape. Using some dark brown yarn and a chenille needle, attach the snout to the head by piercing through the snout and embroidering two vertical stitches for the nose.

Materials

Small amounts of 4-ply (fingering) yarn in pale pink and dark brown
Small amount of beige felting fleece
Two 4mm (⅛in) black beads
Black cotton thread

Tools

35mm (1⅜in) and 45mm (1¾in) pompom makers
Patchwork scissors
Felting needle
Needle felting mat
Chenille needle
Sewing needle

Size

6cm (2¼in)

Templates

Ear

Arm

Snout

Leave loose fibres where dotted lines are shown.

9 Attach the eye beads (see page 26 for instructions on attaching eyes).

Duck & Duckling

Instructions

Duck

1 For the head, make a pompom using the 25mm (1in) pompom maker and white yarn. Tie the centre and finish the pompom. Leave a long yarn tail.

2 For the body, make two pompoms using the 35mm (1⅜in) and 45mm (1¾in) pompom makers in white yarn. Tie the centre and finish the pompoms. Leave long yarn tails.

3 Attach the three pompoms to one another using the yarn tails. Position the pompoms slightly off-centre, using the photograph for guidance. Draw the yarn tight to connect the pompoms securely. Trim the Duck to shape.

4 For the beak, take a small amount of yellow felting fleece and roll it into 2 x 3cm (¾ x 1¼in) loose, flat ball. Stab it with a felting needle, matching it to the template. Lift the fleece from time to time so that the piece doesn't stick to the mat. Leave some fibres trailing from the straight edge.

5 Attach the beak to the face, working the loose fibres into the pompom.

6 For the feet, work as for step 4 to make two feet, matching them to the shape of the template. Attach the feet to the body, working the loose fibres into the pompom.

7 Attach the eye beads using black cotton thread (see page 26 for instructions on attaching eyes).

Duckling

1 For the head and body, make a dense pompom using the 25mm (1in) pompom maker and soft yellow yarn. Trim the pompom to create the head and body.

2 For the beak, cut some yellow felt to the shape of the template. Using a fine sewing needle and yellow cotton thread, attach the beak to the face by threading through the flat edge of the beak and sewing it into a downward curve.

3 Attach the eye beads as for the Duck.

Materials

To make both:

Small amounts of 4-ply (fingering) yarn in white and soft yellow

Small amount of yellow felting fleece

Two 2mm (1/16in) and two 4mm (1/8in) black beads

Black and yellow cotton thread

Small amount of yellow felt

Tools

25mm (1in), 35mm (1⅜in) and 45mm (1¾in) pompom makers

Patchwork scissors

Felting needle

Needle felting mat

Chenille needle

Sewing needle

Size

Duck: 7cm (2¾in); Duckling: 3cm (1¼in)

Templates

Duck's beak

Duck's foot

Duckling's beak

Leave loose fibres where dotted lines are shown.

Hummingbird

Instructions

1 For the head, make a pompom using the 25mm (1in) pompom maker. Wind the top third of the first arm in orange yarn. Wrap the rest in green yarn until the arm is full. Wind the second arm in green yarn until it is full. Tie the centre and finish the pompom.

First arm   *Second arm*

2 For the body, make a pompom using the 35mm (1⅜in) pompom maker. Wind the top third of the first arm in white yarn. Wrap the rest in green yarn until it is full. Wind the second arm in green yarn until it is full. Tie the centre and finish the pompom. Leave a long yarn tail.

First arm   *Second arm*

Templates

Tail & Wing

Beak

Leave loose fibres where dotted line is shown.

Leave a yarn tail as shown.

Materials

Small amounts of 4-ply (fingering) yarn in green, orange and white
Small amount of dark brown felting fleece
Two 4mm (⅛in) black beads
Black cotton thread

Tools

25mm (1in) and 35mm (1⅜in) pompom makers
Patchwork scissors
Felting needle
Needle felting mat
Chenille needle
Sewing needle

Size

6cm (2¼in)

3 Attach the two pompoms to each other using the yarn tails. Refer to the photograph for guidance on colour positioning. Draw the yarn tight to connect the two pompoms securely. Trim the Hummingbird to shape.

4 For the wings and the tail, wind some green yarn around two fingers ten times, release and place it onto a felting mat, leaving a long yarn tail. Stab it with a felting needle until the yarn knits together and the wing matches the shape of the template. Repeat twice more. Attach the wings and tail to the body, using the yarn tails (see page 30 for instructions on making and attaching features with yarn).

5 For the beak, place a strip of dark brown felting fleece onto the felting mat and felt it into a stick shape, matching it to the shape of the template. Leave some loose fibres at the flat edge. Attach the beak to the head, working the loose fibres into the pompom.

6 Attach the eye beads (see page 26 for instructions on attaching eyes).

Crab & Hermit Crab

Materials

To make both:

Small amounts of 4-ply (fingering) yarn in red and sandy brown

Four 5mm (³⁄₁₆in) black beads

Black cotton thread

Tools

20mm (³⁄₄in) and 25mm (1in) pompom makers

Patchwork scissors

Felting needle

Needle felting mat

Chenille needle

Sewing needle

Size

3cm (1¼in)

Instructions

Crab

1 For the body, make a pompom using the 25mm (1in) pompom maker and red yarn.

2 For the legs, wind some red yarn around your forefinger five times, release and place it onto a felting mat. Stab it with a felting needle until the yarn knits together into a slightly elongated ball shape. Leave a long yarn tail. Repeat for the other seven legs. Attach them to the body, using the yarn tails (see page 30 for instructions on making and attaching features with yarn).

3 For the large pincer, wind some red yarn around your forefinger ten times. Release and place it onto a felting mat. Stab it with a felting needle. Shape the yarn into a flat, round piece and cut a segment out of the centre with scissors. Repeat for the small pincer, winding the yarn around your forefinger eight times. Attach the pincers to the body, using the yarn tails.

4 Attach the eye beads (see page 26 for instructions on attaching eyes).

Templates

Crab

Large pincer

Small pincer

Leave yarn tails as shown.

Instructions

Hermit Crab

1 For the head, make a pompom using the 20mm (¾in) pompom maker and red yarn.

2 For the shell, make two pompoms using the 25mm (1in) pompom maker and sandy brown yarn, leaving long yarn tails. Trim and shape one of them so that it is slightly smaller than the other. Make one more pompom with the 20mm (¾in) pompom maker and sandy brown yarn. Connect the three pompoms using the yarn tails, placing the smallest at one end. Draw the yarn tight to connect the pompoms securely. Trim the shell to shape.

3 Attach the head pompom to the shell at the larger pompom end.

4 Make pincers as for the Crab. Wind some red yarn fifteen times and ten times respectively for large and small pincers. Leave long yarn tails. Attach them to the body, using the yarn tails.

5 Attach the eye beads (see page 26 for instructions on attaching eyes).

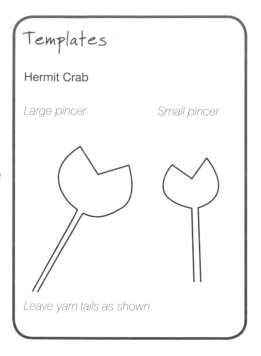

Templates

Hermit Crab

Large pincer   *Small pincer*

Leave yarn tails as shown.

Ostrich

Instructions

1 For the head, make a pompom using the 25mm (1in) pompom maker and either pink or blue yarn. Leave a long yarn tail.

2 For the body, make a pompom using the 45mm (1¾in) pompom maker and either pink or blue yarn. Leave a long yarn tail.

3 For the beak, take a small amount of yellow felting fleece and felt it into a small cone shape. Leave loose fibres trailing from the straight edge. Attach the beak to the face, working the loose fibres into the pompom.

4 Attach the eye beads (see page 26 for instructions on attaching eyes).

5 For the neck, place some beige felting fleece about 6cm (2¼in) long on the mat. Stab it with a needle and roll it into a stick shape. Lift the fleece from time to time so that the piece doesn't stick to the mat. Work until it is fairly firm.

Materials

To make one:

Small amounts of DK (8-ply/light worsted) yarn in pink or blue

Small amount of dark brown, beige and yellow felting fleece

Two 4mm (⅛in) black beads

Black cotton thread

Tools

25mm (1in) and 45mm (1¾in) pompom makers
Patchwork scissors
Felting needle
Needle felting mat
Chenille needle
Sewing needle

Size

8.5cm (3¼in) sitting height

Templates

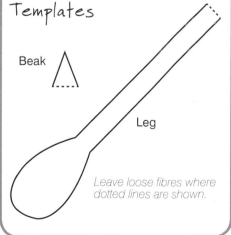

Beak

Leg

Leave loose fibres where dotted lines are shown.

6 For the legs, take a long strip of dark brown felting fleece and roll the end section into 2 x 3cm (¾ x 1¼in) loose, flat ball (see above right). Place it onto a felting mat and stab it with a felting needle, matching it to the shape of the template (see right). Continue felting the leg, rolling the fleece into a stick shape. Bend the leg at the ankle and felt the ankle to shape (see below right). Attach the legs to the body by felting the loose fibres into the pompom.

7 To connect the head to the body, thread the yarn tail from the body through the felted neck and up through the head and back again. You could also use the yarn tail from the head to go the other way, to make it extra secure. Hide the yarn ends inside the pompoms.

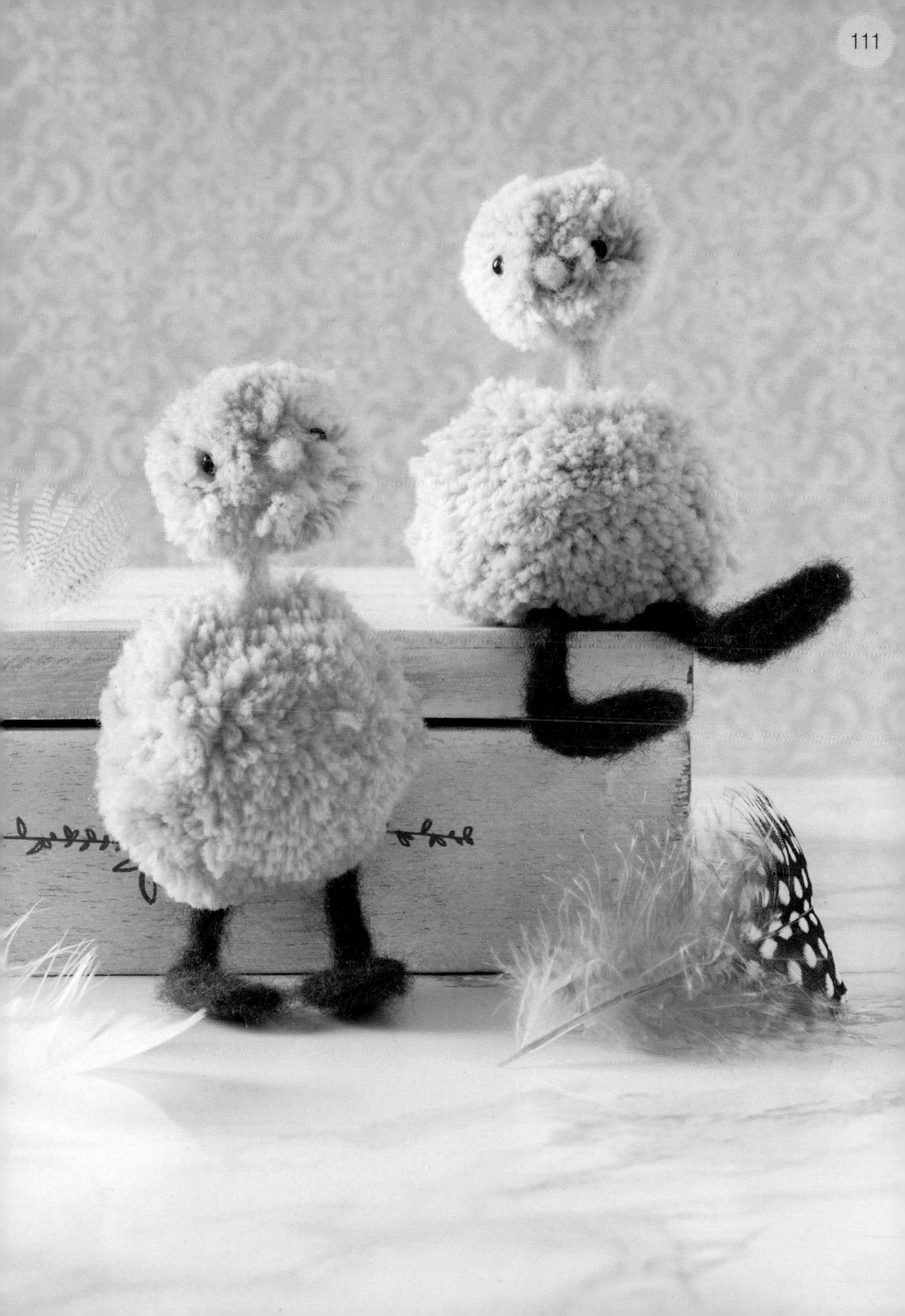

Index